Alfred H Wall

Artistic Landscape Photography

Alfred H Wall

Artistic Landscape Photography

ISBN/EAN: 9783744666237

Printed in Europe, USA, Canada, Australia, Japan

Cover: Foto ©Thomas Meinert / pixelio.de

More available books at **www.hansebooks.com**

ARTISTIC
LANDSCAPE
PHOTOGRAPHY

A SERIES OF CHAPTERS ON THE
PRACTICAL AND THEORETICAL PRINCIPLES OF
PICTORIAL COMPOSITION.

BY

A. H. WALL.

Author of
"Stray Chapters on Art," "The Technology of Art,"
"Harmonious Colouring," etc.

Formerly Editor of
"The Art Student," and "The Illustrated Photographer."

PERCY LUND & CO., LTD., THE COUNTRY PRESS, BRADFORD;
AND MEMORIAL HALL, LONDON, E.C.

CONTENTS.

CHAPTER I.
PRELIMINARY 9

CHAPTER II.
ON THOUGHT AND OBSERVATION AS THE FOUNDATIONS OF SUCCESS IN ART 21

CHAPTER III.
ON THE IMAGINATION AND ITS CULTIVATION 29

CHAPTER IV.
ABOUT TRUTHFULNESS IN ART 39

CHAPTER V.
ON THE EXPRESSION OF SPACE 51

CHAPTER VI.
ON SKIES, CLOUDS, AERIAL PERSPECTIVE AND ATMOSPHERIC EFFECTS 61

CHAPTER VII.
ON WATER AS AN ELEMENT OF PICTORIAL EFFECT 93

CHAPTER VIII.
OF SENTIMENT AND FEELING, CONTRASTS AND VARIETY, SUBORDINATION, DOMINATION AND HARMONY .. 105

CHAPTER IX.
PICTORIAL COMPOSITION 115

CHAPTER X.
THE COMPOSITION OF OUTLINES, AND THE POINTS OF VIEW   127

CHAPTER XI.
PERSPECTIVE, PHOTOGRAPHICAL AND PICTORIAL   137

CHAPTER XII.
BREADTH OF EFFECT   151

CHAPTER XIII.
FIGURES AND FOREGROUNDS   163

CHAPTER XIV.
GOOD HINTS FROM GOOD AUTHORITIES OLD AND NEW   .. 169

PREFACE.

THE art possibilities of photography, although fairly demonstrated, are not yet fairly recognised, or sought after. How to use the camera and chemicals is not all the knowledge required by a photographer to make him an artist, any more than knowing how to use pigments and brushes is all a painter requires to produce pictures. To "take" a mere ordinary photograph is a simple easy task, to produce by photography a genuine picture is quite another thing.

In the following chapters I address beginners in art, who, although they may be accomplished photographers, are not artistic, and if to certain sections of my readers I appear too didactic I trust they will remember that I am addressing not only advanced students but also the young in art, including the veriest tyros.

Some of the chapters included in this volume have already appeared in *The Practical Photographer* and *The Amateur Photographer*, but each has been carefully revised, added to, and for the most part re-written.

A. H. W.

Stratford-on-Avon, 1896.

CHAPTER I.

PRELIMINARY.

> "He who does not ascertain what a picture is before he attempts to produce it is like one who runs a race without knowing either the course or the goal." —*The Art Student.*

THERE is a steadily widening field for photographic work of the better kind, and a very promising field of study for those who desire to elevate its artistic pretensions. But, unfortunately, it is so easy for anyone to carry a camera, expose a plate and either develop or get it developed, that a vast quantity of the poorest productions at once lowers the dignity and importance of it as art-work, and makes the pretensions of most photographers to take rank with artists, simply ludicrous. But photography is not the only calling that exhibits high and low class work, that has in its ranks practitioners of talent and intellect, and others who lack both plentifully.

Artists of eminence have frankly admitted the possibility of producing photographic pictures (but only when the photographer is also the artist) because they have taken trouble to understand the possibilities of the camera and seen them illustrated. Other artists, as eminent but less reasonable, still continue to deny *all* photographers the power of producing pictures, refusing to listen to argument or see what they don't want to see.

Then there are photographers of the old school in

whose eyes any photograph that is "sharp," full of microscopically minute detail and free from distortion, however uninteresting and commonplace its subject and inartistic its treatment, is superior to all other pictures. And so it is with press critics who do not understand either the principles of art or the power and capabilities of photography.

Again there are those who understand art but not photography. An amusing illustration will be found in that exceedingly valuable and interesting work, the late Mr. Hammerton's *Painter's Tour in the Highlands*, in which faults due to common blunders of manipulation and judgment are seriously advanced as arguments conclusively demonstrating the necessarily inartistic character of *all* photographs. It would have been as just to deny the ability of Sir Joshua Reynolds to produce a picture because such miserable daubs were painted by cheap portraitists, using the brushes and the oil colours with which he produced his pictures.

Another way of regarding our subject is seen in the rapidly increasing number of professional photographers who can only support themselves by lowering prices. Art culture and practice are of course out of the question in their case. These mechanical, cheap operators, with their ignoble self-content, neither read nor think, they stagnate. But worst of all they drive out of the calling men who would love, honour and ennoble it, students of refined and elevated taste, acquainted with both science and art.

The fact that a large number of the best pictorial photographs are "taken" by amateurs, who have ambition, learning and leisure, is a very hopeful sign. Where they lead others will follow; and where they enter into competition with professional operators on the walls of our exhibitions, the standard is sure to rise year by year, and photography to rise with it in public estimation.

Hopeful signs for the future of pictorial photography exist in new fields of activity. Nearly all the illustrated papers and magazines now use photographs for automatic engraving processes. We have a new Art Society's Exhibition of works judged only as pictures, separating purely photographic art study from its apparatus and materials and its more purely scientific and mechanical applications, just as the study of painting, sculpture, architecture and music are separated from the chemistry and manufacture of pigments and pencils, the making of brushes and easels, and the manufacturing of fiddles, etc.

And, side by side with these wholesome changes, we have that growing demand for more thoroughly systematic art instruction to which the following chapters owe their existence. In what form this can be best and most usefully given is now the question, a reply to which is suggested by the success which has attended the delivery and publication of lectures at the Royal Academy of Fine Arts ever since it was founded; in the reading of papers written by artists for artists at the meetings of photographic societies; and the fact that these lectures and papers have always been most permanently useful when printed and published.

But it must not be concluded that our photographic method of producing pictures is, however, on all fours with the painter's. The rules by which the painter works will not suffice for the photographer's guidance, because their preliminary training is necessarily not the same. In the painter's education, drawing, anatomy, perspective and the principles of pictorial composition, train his eye and hand, inform his mind and establish principles before he attempts to master the more mechanical elements of composition, as otherwise he would find them misleading and confusing. Moreover, as an old artist and fellow student of mine (Scarlet F. Potter, art critic, sculptor and poet) once said:—" All of us, considered as men, are doubtless improved by having the imagination cultured, the mind refined, and the moral principles raised and strengthened; but all are not by such means better fitted for the discharge of their professional duties. It is a hard necessity of civilized life that the man must be subordinated to the part he fills in the great social machine. But we, as artists, have fortunately one advantage over our fellows, for the more fully we can develop the individual man, the more likely are we to excel in art." In the nineteenth century we recognise the truth of this; but in the eighteenth, as James Barry, R.A., says:—" A great number of works of very limited merit were produced, in which all academical rules of composition, drawing and *chiaro oscuro* were strictly observed, which, notwithstanding, appear only as well-executed exercises, and leave the spectator cold, because they are wanting in the first and most indispensable attributes of works of art, namely, the expressions of the vivid individual feeling of the artist, which show the real soul of a work of art." All the fervour which means power, all the thought which creates ambition and fully develops the perceptive faculties, come from intellectual as distinct from technical and mechanical studies. Because the artists of Greece were highly cultured, intellectual men (says the great artist above quoted, in his academy lecture on "Design"), and because they were "familiarised to the most subtle and refined philosophy, and appear to have considered the whole of created nature" as elements of study; we have "all those masterly works of poetry, painting, and sculpture" which have for thousands of years "filled the mind with astonishment, instruction and pleasure, and which will ever remain unequalled by those who do not draw their materials from the same source." Again he emphatically repeats, "the superiority of the ancient Greeks over the moderns arose entirely from moral causes, and principally from the advantages of their education."

These remarks are not more applicable to the highest forms of fine art than they are to the humblest. They are those of a practised artist who said what he felt and knew to be true. His words are as applicable to photography as they are to painting, sculpture and architecture. True art-work is not the producing of mere dumb, lifeless outer-seemings, "which are indeed but seeming!" imitations of hired models, studio accessories and imperfect presentments of nature's soulful loveliness," or those "front elevations" of men and women which we call portraits, or those sunless, airless, uninspiring, uninteresting landscapes we wrongfully call pictures. These are all, whether photographs or paintings, mechanical productions.

Many photographers deny this, and half of them do so as an excuse for working without thinking, with the hands instead of the mind. There was a time, how well I remember it, when, apart from a few photographers who had commenced their careers as painters, any attempt to apply to photography even the simplest principles and rules of art was received with incredulous smiles, or proudly scorned by those who thought it was the mission of photography to do away with art and artists altogether. We know better now, have gone far in advance of that obstinate ignorance and conceit, happily. Most photographers will now, I suppose, acknowledge that at least perspective, composition, and the relative values of tones in light and shade are studies as necessary in photographing as in painting. Barry said of the eighteenth century artists what may be said of certain artist-photographers of to-day, " who leave the spectators cold because they are wanting " in what truly is " the real soul of a work of art," the expression of individual sentiment and feeling.

And here it will not, I think, be uninteresting or useless to glance back and see how art and photography were from the first associated, how art progress in photography was first advocated, how it was retarded and misunderstood, and in what way it began to come once more to the front, until now, when preparations really ought to be made for a fresh attack upon the enemies of artistic photography all along the line.

In very ancient times Science, Poetry, and Art were one. All the great inventions and discoveries of our day had their foreshadowing suggestions in the minds and imaginations of men who died thousands of years ago. But in the comparatively recent days of Lord Bacon, poets, artists and philosophers began to drift apart. The result is that our man of science is, as a rule, no longer imaginative. His bent is materialistic, he deals in solid, square, practical facts, and scorns all "mere" conjectures and deductive reasonings. Everything doubtful he tests by the physical senses, everything that awakens fervid feeling or prompts the play of fancy he regards suspiciously. The poet and artist, although parted, still sympathise with each other as nigh akin, and do so proudly. But the modern man of science generally repudiates the connection more or less scornfully, while those who profess to be scientific without having fairly won their spurs in its glorious domain of strife and conquest, are in this way usually the most aggressively and offensively demonstrative.

Centuries before photography became the practical art-science it now is, poets dreamed of it and philosophers philosophised over it. The first camera-obscura was invented for artists, and the first real photograph ever taken was that of a scientific artist who sought means for realizing the poetical and artistic dream of a long past age.

Chemists and opticians, for the most part, first came into the field as inventors and improvers of photographic tools and materials, after the French painter Daguerre had perfected his invention, and made it that practical reality which France so nobly and generously purchased as a gift for the world, and for which practitioners in England immediately began to take out and squabble over patents.

About the middle of the present century when a large number of trained artists were practising photography they sought the aid of opticians and chemists to improve its pictorial results, and when these new workers took up the process with enthusiasm as fervid as their own, and began to experimentalise and investigate, a bond of union was sought, at first by meeting at each other's studios and private houses, then in connection with the Society of Arts, and lastly, in 1853, by originating "The Photographic Society of Great Britain for the promotion of the Art and Science of Photography, by the interchange of Thought and Experience," a title curiously suggestive of the sixteenth century Art and Science Society founded by the inventor of the camera, Baptista Porta, of Padua.

We owe men of science our grateful thanks for the invaluable assistance they rendered photography in all its sections and departments, and in like way we owe them our best thanks for what they have since done. But when so many of them on the strength of such

16   ARTISTIC LANDSCAPE PHOTOGRAPHY.

services assumed a right of dominance in the photographic societies and journals, as they very soon did, they began to be aggressive and mischievous. It was then only too apparent that they neither understood nor appreciated pictorial art, that they regarded sentiment, feeling and imagination as matters with which photography had nothing whatever to do, and artists as mischievous meddlers, and mere impracticable, visionary dreamers.

Yet the first President of the first Photographic Society was Sir Charles Eastlake, who was also President of the Royal Academy of Fine Arts.* He accepted office with the idea that students of photography would also be art students; that the training of a camera student in picture photographing and that of a student of picture painting would differ mainly in technical matters and the resulting effects, but that forming a taste for art excellence and teaching its principles would be as legitimately the work of the Photographic Society as it was that of the Royal Academy. Unluckily this idea found no supporters amongst scientific photographers — they laughed it to scorn — and, consequently, Sir Charles Eastlake, Sir William Newton, Roger Fenton (its first secretary), and artists generally soon lost interest in their proceedings.

Sir William Newton was one of photography's earliest practitioners and experimentalists, and the first Photographic Society's first Vice-President. He had

* Mr. John Leighton, F.S.A., who was one of the founders of this society and read one of the first of its papers, contrasting nature and art in the productions of both painters and photographers, of which only a brief extract was printed, writing recently to the editor of *The Practical Photographer*, said, " In those days the Photographic Society was artistic. Roger Fenton, the secretary, being in the first place a painter, and in the second a photographer," adding, " as artists we were at that period greatly interested in pictorial effect and binocular photography."

played a prominent part in the meetings which originated it, and was famous as a miniature painter. His was the first paper read before the first ordinary meeting. It was " Upon Photography in an Artistic View, and its Relation to the Arts." In it he urged that photographs should be ranked and criticised as pictures, and be, not only optically and chemically wonderful, but artistically beautiful. "The camera," said he, "is itself by no means calculated to teach the principles of art, although *to those* who are already well informed in this respect, it may be made the means of considerable advancement." He then very courteously and carefully pointed out certain shortcomings in perspective and pictorial effect in ordinary photographs, which he called upon all present to unite in attacking, as destructive alike to truthful representation and pictorial beauty. He referred with regret to views held by some scientific gentlemen then present, who asserted that "a photograph should always remain as it was in the camera," without any attempt being made to test its truthfulness or give it artistic merit. Their argument—as afterwards openly stated by one of their number, an amateur photographer, chemical experimentalist and microscopist, who for some years edited *The British Journal of Photography* — was that photography was superior to all art in both its truthfulness and its beauty. "The scientific man," said he, "does not accept art for art, but art for science; he does not like to have the representation of a natural object made so perfectly beautiful that no one would recognise it."* And most of the scientists present endorsed his words.

* This idea of beauty being artificial, and natural objects not beautiful, is a very curious, wide-spread, vulgar blunder, which writers and thinkers of the highest rank have often endeavoured to expose.

B

Since these remarks were foolishly spoken, great changes have been wrought. The question, Should photography be practised artistically? has been discussed over and over again. from all points of view, and the test of a photograph is now almost invariably the pictorial one.

As long ago as 1860 I wrote—" Photography should stand as high in the domain of art as it does in that of science ; and its professors should consider the principles and theories of learned painters, as legitimate a branch of study as either optics or chemistry."* Looked at in an impartial way, and from a common sense point of view, all work takes rank as high or low, mental or mechanical, not by virtue of its tools, materials and process, but by virtue of elements which the worker puts into it. Work that never rises to the intellectual standard is not, and never can be fine art work. Shakespeare himself could not put into the making of a chair or table what he put into his poems and plays. But work which affords scope and finds exercise for superior knowledge, taste and intellectual power, which appeals to the heart and makes it feel, or to the mind and creates thought and imagination, is fine art whether it be produced through the agency of pigments and brushes, or cameras, chemicals and lenses.

But the truest test of photography as an art process is not theoretical ; it is practical. In every succeeding annual exhibition of the Photographic Societies the number of works having genuine artistic merit and pictorial beauty has of late increased, and is still slowly increasing, although for years the dead level of sameness and mediocrity, so characteristic of stagnation, was invariably present.

* " Harmonious Colouring," by A. H. Wall.

During all the years of dominant scientific government in the societies and journals, when opticians saw in photographs the means of demonstrating optical principles and the perfection of their lenses only, and chemists, merely the results of their chemical experiments and theories, artists could only speak for themselves at the exhibitions. But gradually, very gradually, the original idea of the inventors of the camera and the daguerreotype, and that of the artist section of the founders of the first photographic society, has been reasserting itself. Its growth is, however, not yet free and unimpeded. Weeds still check its full elevation and wholesome development. But the soil is being gradually cleared and made ready for the reception of the good seed, and the sowers are not wanting. Sentiment, feeling, and methods of expressing, including pictorial composition, perspective, and the practical association of the imaginative with the actual, are all receiving attention.

Nothing but artistic and poetic good can come of such studies, and so we turn from this backward glance to look forward, full of hopefulness and ambitious aspirations.

It is some time since G. A. Story, A.R.A., wrote: —" It appears that there is a sort of rivalry between photographers and artists, that they, as it were, stand opposite to each other like two armies in battle array. They have thrown down the gauntlet, and will soon be rushing together, but I see no reason why it should not be to shake hands, for I feel sure they are mutually of the greatest services to each other. Photography could not trace the footprints of the beautiful if art did not leave those footprints in her track, neither could it make its own pictures so perfect but for the lessons of art, and the artistic feelings that point the camera."

CHAPTER II.

ON THOUGHT AND OBSERVATION AS THE FOUNDATIONS OF SUCCESS IN ART.

LIGHT and shade being the means whereby we depict surfaces and forms in a photograph, any carelessness in the exposure of a plate, any differences in the tones of a print as compared with those of nature, indicate, in one way or another, untruthfulness. If the intermediate tones are not true, neither are the shapes or surfaces, the light or the shade, or the atmosphere. In many negatives the highest light is always as intense as it can be, and the deepest shadow *always* as nearly as possible black, whether the illuminating conditions were those of brilliant sunlight, soft grey daylight, a semi-misty sunrise or the solemn glory of a gorgeous sunset. In each such case the scale of tones and the gradations of light and shade are false. Again, in how many photographs do we see the highest light in a foreground represented by pure white, and the highest light of some object which should have half-a-mile of atmosphere between it and us quite as white. Can this be true in tone or perspective? Is it not a discord in the harmony of natural beauty? Does not the mere fact of such a blunder being possible in itself demonstrate the necessity for photographers to acquire accurate observation and artistic culture?

How often, again, do we see the white sunlit sail of a boat on a lake and the flash of sunlight on the water both rendered in a photograph by patches of pure empty white, as if the whiteness of the one and that of the other had no difference in intensity. Such is mechanical work, and if you put art "to a mechanical use," says John Ruskin, "you destroy it at once."

It is with the mind that we see, hear and feel, and by cultivating it we develop and give new power to the senses with which it is so mysteriously associated. If it were not so, animals with organs of vision and hearing far superior to ours, such as we find in the very lowest forms of creation, would be our intellectual superiors, knowing more because they can see and hear with greater accuracy and perfection. It is here, as elsewhere, not the tools, but the superior skill and knowledge of the tool maker and the tool user that give the best results.

In making a departure from the ordinary course of teaching, I here want to impress upon you that although good materials and perfect apparatus are very important, the arts of using them are at least no less. For with even the best of all mechanism, we cannot afford to let reason rust idly within that other impenetrable mystery named brain, which, to speak sooth, has apparently about as much to do with thinking as the eye has with perceiving.

"Vision," says a popular art teacher, "like any other faculty, requires cultivation. We must see clearly and perceive truly to depict forcibly and justly. For want of this cultivation of eye and mind, thousands pass through life without knowing that they seldom see a superficies, and never a solid, except a globe, with its true form. It is not, therefore, because our eyes are open, that we see, the mind requires to be furnished with some means from the exercise of which the eye is enabled to judge accurately of form," etc.

But between the complicated sensation we call seeing, and that of obtaining what we call optical or

Composition of Wood and Water.
From a Photograph by Prince Bara Thakoor.

camera images there is indeed very slight relationship, and this we desire to impress upon students at this early stage of our progress, that they may have more justly appreciative, more definite and accurate ideas of the mission and purposes of pictorial art.

Mr. George Wall, in his very able and deeply interesting book, " The Natural History of Thought," says, " External objects being perceived by means of impressions on the sensorium depend upon the proficiency acquired in the use of the organs of sense, and in the power of the perceptive faculty itself. Hence the baby's first ideas of external objects must be of uncertain character and very weak. For this reason many repetitions and much tentative effort must be required before it can attain any clear definite ideas. It is doubtful," he adds, " whether objects are even recognised as external until memory and reflection aid the perception," and again, as he says, " even the simplest images of vision are associated with ideas of distance, dimension and other relations *of a purely intellectual character.*"

The image-conveying lens differs from the idea-conveying sense in other ways. What a madman sees, or his nearest kin, a drunkard in the awful grip of D.T., may have little or no connection with external objects, but even if a lens has had a glass too much its consequent distortions are altogether dependent upon external objects. With these thoughts in view I think beginners in art studies will perceive that the cultivation of their perceptive faculties should be their first business, whether they are disciples of the palette or the camera. Put aside then the false notion that the productions of photography are *of necessity* truthful and beautiful. Remember, then, that as drawing is to the painter the grammar of his art, so accurate perception is to the photographer the test of his art.

It cannot be too frequently or too emphatically stated that whatever process it comes from, a work of art is good or bad, high or low, in exact proportion to the amount of perceptive and intellectual work with which it is associated. The combined operations of the optician, chemist, maker of apparatus and manipulator should in every way possible be subordinated to the purpose of the artist. The photographer who sets up his camera directed by no properly developed perceptive powers, will not, except at long intervals and by some lucky chance which he does not appreciate or recognise, produce a picture. He knows nothing of originality in conception, selection or execution. Nothing—except it be that vanity which is begotten by ignorance—inspires his ambition or warms him into fervour, and his productions are just such dull, poor, commonplace things as Tom, Jack and Harry are producing in countless thousands all over the country, and selling at prices which barely suffice to feed and clothe their wives and families and keep a roof above their heads. Paintings and photographs are alike in this. They are artistic when mental culture and a knowledge of art principles govern their creation, they are inartistic when produced without mental effort or artistic knowledge.

I have quoted Sir William Newton's remarks on the art status of photography in 1853, from an article on this subject in a "Quarterly Review" of 1865. Allow me now to show that what he said, because he spoke truly, is still in harmonious accordance with what another able thinker, Sir Howard Grubb, recently said at Dublin. "In the early days of photography," said he, "a photographer never thought it worth his while to point his camera to any object that had not some particular interest connected with it. It might be a building having historical interest, or architectural beauty, or it might be a well-known and favoured landscape celebrated far and wide for its beauty; the aim, in fact, of the photographer at that time was to produce a representation, or we might say, a portrait of some particular object which had a special interest in itself; but what photographer of that time would have thought of wasting his plates—as it would have been considered —in pointing his camera to those little bits of moor or fen, or some nameless brook, out of which the modern photographer has produced his most exquisite pictures. I say pictures advisedly, because that is just the difference between the photographs of the present day and the photographs of the past. The superiority of the later efforts of photographers depended much more on the fact that, whereas in former time the photographer's aim was to produce a representation or a portrait of a particular scene, that of the modern photographer is to produce a picture."

This is so fully illustrated in recent photographic exhibitions that it is difficult to understand why the literature of photography should not march with the times, and progress in both theory and practice with the rapidly increasing number of artist practitioners and the thousands who, being desirous of doing genuine artistic work, are now asking for the aid of capable instructors. It cannot be too frequently or emphatically stated that in all its best qualities, and however it is produced, a real picture is the outcome, not of a mechanical process but of intellectual study. The photographer who sets up a camera directed by no appreciation of the picturesque and poetical, who is governed by no knowledge of pictorial arts and its scientific principles, is no more an artist than the painter is who, with thought unawakened, imagination unaffected, and heart untouched, in a like way puts up his easel, although each may be truly clever and display great technical knowledge and manual dexterity.

In saying so much we are saying nothing new, only something that should be better known or appreciated amongst those whose words and works betray either their entire ignorance of such matters; or a careless disregard. We want you to see those principles which are the foundation stones of art in all its noblest and loftiest aims, to build upon them in your practice, to recognise what you have to avoid, and what you must acquire before you can produce pictorial photographs which will do honour to yourself and your art. Ruskin says that in training young artists we should "take care that their minds receive such training that they shall see and feel the noblest things," and adds, "of all parts of an artist's education this is the most neglected." Thought and observation are indeed the foundation of success in art, and these must be developed and cultivated systematically and carefully by self-education; but apart from this, which is true in a general sense, there are other things of special value which we shall proceed to speak of separately.

CHAPTER III.

ON THE IMAGINATION AND ITS CULTIVATION.

> The world is full of poetry—the air
> Is living with its spirit; and the waves
> Dance to the music of its melodies,
> And sparkle in its brightness. Earth is veiled
> And mantled with its beauty.—*Percival*.

"BY the culture of imagination," says Henry Reed (a former professor in the University of Pennsylvania), "I mean not such a faculty of the mind as gives birth to common works of fiction, not even such as is represented in the inadequate analysis that is met with in the usual systems of metaphysics, but that creative power which, whether it bear the name of imagination or no, is an element of every great mind. I mean that inventive wisdom which brings the truth to life by the help of its own creative energy in the souls of mighty artists, whether their art be poetry, or painting or sculpture."

"Cultivate the imagination," says G. J. Goschen, "to introduce you to wider and nobler fields of thought." And another writer on the same subject, who was living in 1831, says, "The imagination is nothing more than the mental education by which, and by thought and reading, every student is enabled to exercise some species of talent, and without which an artist will never rise beyond the mechanic who does a thing as he is taught to do it, and who only knows the one way of doing it, and by one particular process. Such men are not artists, though they bear the name."

I am somewhat given to quoting men of acknowledged ability, and sometimes take great pains to ascertain their opinions, as my readers well know ; and when their endorsement strengthens my argument or illustrates my meaning, I do not see why I should not quote them.

The purpose of this chapter may strike some of my readers as far-fetched and fantastic, for people commonly regard imagined things as unreal, and therefore altogether outside the domain of photography. But let us briefly examine a few positive facts, and follow them up to their legitimate logical deductions, and the result may be a change of opinion. " Of all mysteries," says an author I have already quoted, Mr. George Wall, "none except the supreme mystery, God himself, is greater or more inscrutable, or at any time more real and influential than the faculty of thinking. . . . . And of all our mental faculties, imagination is one of the most mysterious. By its aid we see without eyes, hear without ears, feel without the mechanism of touch. It stirs our feelings, creates our thoughts, gives our ideas force, reality and vitality. To appeal to it successfully is the work of our greatest thinkers, our most eloquent speakers, our most accomplished artists." Dr. Johnson in his famous Dictionary says imagination means " The power of forming ideal pictures, the power of representing absent things to ourselves and others." Well, that is just what both painting, poetry and photography do. The definition is, however, hardly comprehensive enough. A faculty which in its operation links together the writings of historians, travellers, poets, dramatists, novelists, etc., etc. (for they all present to the mental eye things invisible to the outer eye), in like way links together the painter, sculptor, actor and photographer, because each in his respective way also realizes absent things.

Mr. G. J. Goschen (M.P.), in his admirable and useful little book called the "Cultivation and Use of Imagination," says, "Its development by suitable studies enables us to live, move and think in a world different from the narrow world surrounding us, to have the heart as well as the intellect stirred, to have our sympathies expanded, our source of happiness enlarged, our means of enjoyment increased in number, our moral characters improved." If, therefore, photography can appeal to, and develop imagination, it is doing noble work. If its pictorial productions can be seen without feeling, or without awakening interest forcible enough to act upon the imagination, it is doing ignoble work.

Your solid, dull, coldly unsympathetic, unemotional man or woman will neither respond to any appeal made to their imaginations, or make any appeal to the imaginations of other people. More than half the joys of living are lost to them. How many of them are now taking photographs in every way like themselves. The man, Peter, whom Wordsworth depicted as untouched by nature's beauty, incapable of recognising poetical or other associations, to whom a primrose by the river's brim

"A yellow primrose was to him,
And it was nothing more,"

merely a word, a name, and therefore exceedingly uninteresting. Yet Peter would probably have taken a very decent photograph if some one had but shown him how to use a camera. But because he could neither see nor appreciate beauty, because Nature's loveliness "did never melt into his heart," and because "He never felt the witchery of the soft blue sky," his photograph would be simply a photograph, certainly not a picture.

Where does the painter of landscapes differ most from the mechanical landscape photographer? Is it not in choice, selection and treatment of subject? The ordinary camera man sees what he wants almost at a glance, and straightway plants his tripod at the usual height, elevates his camera and looks to its levelling, focusses to secure equal sharpness of detail on every plane, near or distant, and in every object, whether of dominant or subordinate interest; regulates his exposure

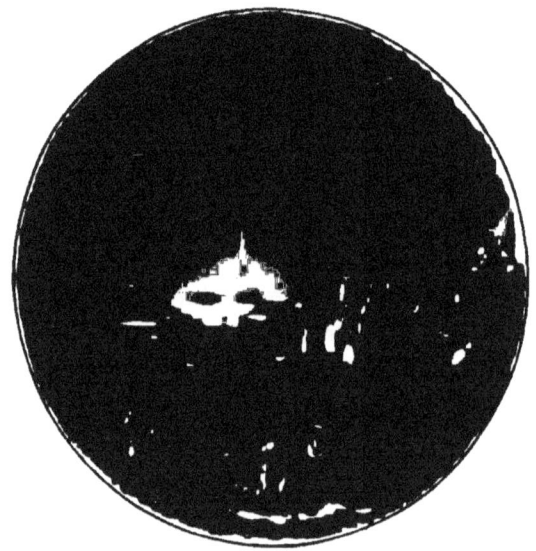

Uses of Foreground Figures.

and development with ideas in no way suggested by pictorial intentions, imaginative conceptions, or poetical sentiments. He is in every way the slave of his tools. Even the shape and size of his picture is not suggested by him or its character, but by the size of his plate and the opening of his mounting cards. And as he seeks a subject, so he exposes his plate, with his heart untouched, his thinking powers inactive; and, closing the shutter, he packs his traps and marches away, perfectly

THE IMAGINATION AND ITS CULTIVATION. 33

happy and contented, proud to think that he can "take a picture" and call himself "an artist."

But the artistic or imaginative man, the thinker, the man of feeling, acts very differently. He sees the selected view at various times, under differing conditions of light and atmosphere, carefully determines what shape and size will be best for it in connection with the means he has to work with, and all he desires to include in the view, and also what he desires to exclude. He

Foreground Figures.

tries various points of view: now higher, now lower; now to this side, now to that; sometimes backward, sometimes forward; his thought all the time busy with the principles of harmony, variety, contrasts; considering the value of tones in connection with the coming exposure and development, and anxious about obtaining truthfully the expression of air and space, etc. He is on the alert for bits of intense dark and bits of brilliant light to give dominance and prominence to the leading feature, "the Prince of Denmark" in his "Hamlet."

c

He is, in short, on the alert to secure everything which his active imagination and artistic knowledge teaches him to value, everything that will help him to convey desirable ideas forcibly, to awaken in minds and imaginations associated ideas, perceptions and memories, which will deepen the spectator's interest in his work, and make it more nobly and usefully attractive.

When the inartistic operator wants a figure, his assistant or some accidental passer-by serves his purpose, and is asked just to stand here or there, and the thing is done. One figure in one place is as good to him as one in another place, for to him a figure is merely a figure, as to Peter the primrose was but an idealess word.

When the artist has the same want, he lets his mind and imagination go to work. He asks himself what kind of figure would be most appropriately suggestive, how it could be made to tell some kind of story, or best help one already decided upon, or how in what other way it will help the composition, strengthen the governing sentiment, or appeal to the imagination of spectators. He anxiously asks himself whether it should be in light or in shadow; placed here, near the foreground, or there, in the middle distance. If he is a painter, he tries experiments before deciding these questions: puts in and rubs out, tries this way, that way, and the other way, just as the artist photographer would by moving the actual figure and examining effects on his focussing screen. An admirable example of suitable figures suitably used may be seen in a copy from Mr. H. P. Robinson's photograph on the opposite page.

Ruskin, the greatest art teacher of our generation, in his famous "Modern Painters" says, "Only the commonest general truths of nature impress common observers," the people who exercise their perceptive

THE IMAGINATION AND ITS CULTIVATION.   37

powers without previously obtained knowledge or active intellectual power. The casual glance of a careless looker-on conveys to his mind the fewest possible ideas, impresses his memory weakly, and awakens neither his imagination nor sympathetic feelings. He has none of the artist's deeper insights and more thoughtful observings, to impress it forcibly upon his mind.

There is an amusing way of discovering how different seeing is from observing. Ask half-a-dozen ordinary people to describe something which each has

Original Drawing, Showing Figure Taking the Eye
Into the Picture.

seen and each believes he knows perfectly well. They will be sure to disagree, and in some cases probably to a very ludicrous, laughter-provoking extent.

This arises from defective or untrained perceptive powers. We take care that our boys shall have the muscles of their bodies carefully developed and exercised, and boys delight in sports which achieve that development. But the systematic development of our intellectual faculties is not regarded as what it actually is: something of far more serious importance, and equally delightful. If drawing was understood in its full significance as a necessary branch of education, it would be universally regarded as of no less importance than reading and writing. In every phase and stage of our lives, in all our occupations and amusements, what is more important than that power of observing accurately, which gives us so many new pleasures and saves us from committing so many serious blunders? If everybody looked at what they saw as artists do—with the mind's as well as the physical eye—we should have much less self-deception and much more *genuine* imaginative power.

Therefore, to begin with, I say to every photographer who would be an artist, "Cultivate your perceptive powers and the imagination; try to observe carefully and thoughtfully everything you see, for by so doing you develop and strengthen 'the power of forming ideal pictures,' 'the power of representing absent things' to yourselves and to others, feelingly, truthfully and beautifully." "If the imagination of the artist be deficient in vigour, and unable to embody a creation that shall satisfy his understanding and feeling," says the author of "Dogmas in Art," "or if his reasoning be not sound and clear, and his feeling deep and sustained, he will assuredly not satisfy the demands of an authorised critic."

In the power of realizing in Nature outward expressions which appeal most strongly to the imagination through feelings, the photographer will find his opportunities. If his own feelings are untouched by them, his perceptive and imaginative powers are weak, and his chance of success in awakening sympathetic and creative ideas in the minds and hearts of others is very remote and slight.

CHAPER IV.

ABOUT TRUTHFULNESS IN ART.

" True art can only be learned in one school,
and that school is kept by Nature."—*Hogarth*.

" Go, wiser thou ! and in thy scale of sense
Weigh thy opinion against Providence,
Call imperfection what thou fanciest such ;
Say here God gives too little, there too much."—*Pope*.

IT will now be as well, perhaps, to say something practical about what so many regard as the imagination's direct opponent, truthfulness. And here again a quotation from Mr. Goschen's " Cultivation and Use of the Imagination " may help us. He says of certain wildly fanciful and perfectly unreal works of fiction by modern dreamers that they are " lacking in imagination. The constructive faculty has been architectural, *not pictorial* . . . these novelists have eliminated, discarded, dropped too much ;" in other words they distort rather than truthfully represent the real.

Several art-critics, have of late—as already stated—been vigorously active against the graphic claims of photography, because as they affirm it is " too true to nature," and consequently devoid of imaginative power. Thus, " A. U." writing in a London newspaper about one of last year's photographic exhibitions (the Dudley Gallery), speaking of its founders, says : " One of their objects, they announce boldly, is to strengthen and advance the position that photography is making for itself among graphic arts. There could be no greater absurdity; photography may advance and develop and progress; it may have in store for us surprises and inventions innumerable; but it can never be ranked with the graphic arts. I have more than once pointed out the distinction between photography, a mechanical contrivance, and art. But if the men who exhibit here, rest their claims to critical and public interest upon their artistic pretensions, they make it impossible to notice their work and not ignore their ambition to be what they are not. To talk of the drawing made by the sun on the prepared plate is a sad confusion of terms; to vaunt fidelity to Nature as proof of the artistic possibilities of the camera is to misunderstand at the outset the very meaning of art. 'Nature is usually wrong,' Whistler says somewhere; is it for the camera to set her right? A photographer like Mr. George Davison may display much feeling and discrimination in his selection of views to be photographed; but how can he, dependent as he is upon a machine and not upon himself, develop that genius for selection which is exactly what makes the Japanese artist so great? Count Gloeden's photographs of the nude are admirable in every way, but who—save, perhaps, the 'Pictorial Photographer'—would want to class them with the studies of Degas? And if Mr. Hollyer's portraits, as now exemplified by one of Mr. Walter Crane, are admirable, for that reason are they to be placed in the same category as an etching by Rembrandt?"

But is every painter a Rembrandt? And is every painter who is not a Rembrandt, no artist? Answer these questions and the illogical nature of "A. U.'s" argument will at once be visible. If Nature is wrong is it for the easel to set her right? One might imagine in reading such nonsensical statements that only art could make nature beautiful. This curious outcry for the painter to set Nature right, reminds one of the New Hollander's barbarous custom of improving Nature by cutting off the top joint of a finger. It is in vain for " A. U." to tell us that he has " more than once pointed out the distinction between photography, a mechanical science, and art," when he has only asserted the existence of that distinction. Assertions will never prove that the picture or photograph is of necessity the result of tools. Who dreams of tracing bad colouring, false drawing, vulgar treatment and gross ignorance of perspective and anatomy to the use of pigments and brushes? Who will assert that a photograph while expressing faithfully, sympathetically and poetically, Nature's appeal to hearts and minds is not a work of art, because the worker used a camera and chemicals instead of paints and pencils? The mere fact that photographs of the same scene under the same conditions can be produced with strikingly dissimilar results shows how little tools have to do with the matter. Are we to believe that Shakespeare, Milton, Pope, Akenside, Thompson, Wordsworth, Tennyson, and many scores of great poets, who have found in nature perfect loveliness, *may* be mistaken, and Mr. Whistler *may* be right in asserting that " Nature is usually wrong." Is he inevitably right ? It may be true that the photographer is more dependent upon his tools than the painter is, but it has never yet been said of a landscape photograph that the Hanging Committee of any exhibition were unable to decide which was its top and which was its bottom. To admire art as something independent of Nature, and denounce photography as purely mechanical because it does not improve Nature, is indeed going back to the crude, raw beginning of the clumsiest criticism. Is there then no poetry, no romance, nothing that is picture-like in Nature ? Is there no loveliness in woman, no dignity in man, no charm in hill and dale, forest and river, cloud and sky, until they appear upon the painter's canvas? Has the flower we pluck from the garden no beauty compared with its interpretation in paint? Is it indeed "so good" to conclude that photography is, as " A. U." says, merely " a mechanical contrivance," and the photograph ditto? Are the tools, and the productions made with them, on the same ignoble level? Is " fidelity to Nature " no proof of the artistic possibilities of the camera, or the art ability of the painter? Does " A. U.'s " " scathing criticism" reduce us to the deplorable necessity of putting the camera's fidelity on a level with that of nearly all the best artists the world has known? Ruskin says, " Landscape art, should be a witness to the omnipotence of God," not " an exhibition of the dexterity of man"; and he says yet again, "every alteration of the features of Nature has its origin in powerless indolence or blind audacity." And again, " the picture that is painted as a substitute for Nature had better be burned." Our greatest painters, poets and philosophers have all agreed with him in saying " the picture which is looked for as an interpretation of Nature is invaluable."

It is very much easier for such a painter as " A. U." admires to realize his own fantastic and eccentric imaginings than it is to transcribe the facts of Nature into the language of art; easier to make a doll than it is to model a life-like statue. But photography's critics, like doctors, differ widely in their opinions. *The Times*, dealing with the Royal Photographic Society's Exhibition, said, " of late years the claims of photography," in the art direction, " have been persistently urged, and as persistently disputed, and the question does not appear as yet to have found a satisfactory solution. Photographers themselves are not unanimous upon the point;

that is if we may judge from the pronouncements and writings of some of the most prominent members of the society, whose exhibition we are now reviewing. To these there are no possibilities for art in photography. The Photographic Society is not an artistic but rather a scientific society."

Another London newspaper, *The Standard*, said, "it would be flattery to claim that the ordinary amateur helps to any appreciable extent the progress of the art he practises in so mechanical a fashion. But he adds undeniably to the pleasure of his own idle days, and to the instruction of his friends at home. . . . Nor, after glancing through the annual exhibition of the Photographic Society, is it fair to deny the limner, whose partner is the sun, the credit of greatly improving public taste. Take, for example, a photograph from its walls, or, indeed, from the case of any photographer's door, and compare it with the efforts of ten or twenty years ago, and the difference will at once be seen. We do not refer to the really artistic compositions on view, or to the exquisite reproductions of cloud and sea effects, but simply to the pose and costume of the "sitters." The glaring victim bolt upright in front of a crimson curtain, and beside a sham marble pillar, with his forefinger in a book, after the old portrait painter's conventionalism, has vanished. For, when the dress and the attitude of those times appeared in a photograph, the natural result was that they were æstheticised out of existence."

The Daily Telegraph said of the first-named collection, " Advancing by leaps and bounds, the study and science of photography as reflected by an exhibition of the Photographic Society of Great Britain, held in Pall Mall, leaves, apart from the great unsolved problem of colouring, little to be wished for by admirers of the beautiful. Rarely has a more attractive show been held, the high pitch of perfection to which many of the works are brought giving visitors a first impression that they gazed upon delicately-finished water-colours or artistic crayons rather than products of the camera. Every branch of skilful development receives full representation, and where so much is delightful and clever, the judges must have found it a hard task to allot their favours."

A great landscape painter who painted what he saw and not what he imagined he ought to see, John Constable, R.A., in the May of 1809, and a letter to his old friend, John Dunthorne, says: " For the last few years I have been running after pictures and seeking truth at second-hand. I have not endeavoured to represent Nature with the same elevation of mind with which I set out, but have rather tried to make my performances look like the works of other men. I am determined to make no idle visits this summer, nor to give up my time to commonplace people. I shall return to Bergholt, where I shall endeavour to get a pure and unaffected manner of representing the scenes that may employ me. There is little or nothing in the exhibition worth looking up to. There is room enough for a natural painter. The great vice of the present day is *bravura*, an attempt to do something beyond the truth. Fashion always had, and will have, its day; but Truth in all things only will last, and it alone will have just claims on our admiration."

In another letter to another friend he says: " In the early ages of the fine arts the productions were more affecting and sublime, for then the artists, being without human exemplars, were forced to have recourse to Nature."

And, in yet another letter he speaks of " Nature, the mother of all that is valuable in poetry, painting or anything else where an appeal to the soul is required.

The language of the heart is the only one that is universal, and as Sterne says, we should disregard all rules and make our way to the heart as we can."

Fresh testimony to the righteousness of this famous landscape painter's judgment was shown when some of his pictures appeared in the Paris Louvre Gallery, where they had the place of honour, and convinced many of the best French painters that they were all in error—that Nature alone was right, and that a want of fidelity to Nature was a want of artistic power. "Your pictures," said a correspondent, writing to Constable from Paris, "have taught them that *though your means may not be essential*, your end must be to produce an imitation of Nature, and the next exhibition in Paris will teem with your imitators."

Another painter, J. D. Harding, in his " Lessons on Art," enforces this appreciative care, forethought, and delight in Nature for art's sake by saying : " Unless art be studied in conjunction with Nature, a great proportion of the student's intellect and susceptibility must remain 'in Lethe drowned.' Can it be denied that we are so constituted as to enjoy nature, and that nature was intended for our enjoyment ? If not, why need she be beautiful ? Wherefore our esteem of and our running hither and thither to behold her ?"

Let us now change our point of view. A painting or a photograph may represent what the painter or photographer saw faithfully enough so far as regards a few unimportant facts, and yet miss many facts of much greater importance from a pictorial point of view.

" Many," says Mr. G. J. Goschen, " many is the three-volume novel which you can read through from beginning to end while your mind will not be lit up with one spark of imagination. Their authors describe characters precisely similar to the people whom they see every day; they describe the very clothes worn by the people whom they meet every day; they describe the very words which may be addressed to themselves, the very smiles which may be smiled at themselves; they describe the very love which they hope may be made to themselves, or to their sisters; and then at the end they think they have written a novel! Well, that may be fiction, but it is not imagination." In like way photographic views and portraits may be mere outside facts. Many give dead unchangeable masks instead of living faces that seem to breathe and move; flat "front elevations" as apologies for solidity, depth and space; dull uninteresting empty-box facts, instead of complete truths pregnant with thought and feeling. Just as certain facts may be used in argument to uphold glaring falsehoods, and figures made to demonstrate nothing so forcibly as their own unreliability, so in the imitative arts mere reported facts and figures are not necessarily perfect truths. There are such things as inner truths, to which these outside facts belong. To secure the one and miss the other is a very poor kind of success. Yet it contents thousands.

A newspaper report of the murder of Desdemona by a Moor named Othello could put before you, as in a photograph, all the outside facts of that horribly tragic event, but it required a Shakespeare to realize its powerful inner truths. The immobile plaster mask of a beautiful face is a fact entirely, utterly unlike the original face under the influence of stirring thoughts or deep feelings. The mask-face is an imperfect, the face a perfect truth. Earth, air and sky have glorious revelations for the poet painter which the untrained mind cannot perceive, and the uneducated eye cannot see. A well photographed but inartistic landscape gives the outer forms of things accurately enough, but it gives nothing more, it is a mere shell. The newspaper report is looked at for a minute or two and then thrown aside. One does not take it up again and again as if it were a poem to be thought about, or a work of real art, always delightful, always suggesting something new, some fresh beauty, some deeper meaning, or giving us some additional delight.

The photographer has not, it is true, the power an artist possesses in this direction. His tools are different, he works in a different medium, there is not the same full scope for his imagination, but he has a far greater art power than it is commonly said he has. In some respects he has advantages which the artist has not. His colours are not only mixed for him, but are also supplied by science. The purely mechanical work which occupies so large a proportion of the painter's time, in his case occupies very little time. While the painter is laboriously and thoughtfully perfecting one picture, the photographer can turn out scores. But of that which is intellectual, that which is higher, greater and grander as an element of success than all mechanical and technical conditions put together, the photographer may command a fairly good share, if only he will study his calling in a serious, earnest way, and not lightly as if its art possibilities were something of subordinate interest and importance.

One of the earliest things the art student has to acquire is, however, not only the knowledge of what he can do, and should try to do, but the knowledge of what he cannot do, and what it would only be a waste of precious time and energy to struggle for. If he thinks, as some painters do, that he is going to do more than is done by nature, he will waste his time. He is not going to create anything natural, but something artificial. It is the purpose of his art to suggest, not create, not to make the artificial natural, but to seem natural. He has a language purely his own, into which he must translate the truths of nature. He is not a mere transcriber but an interpreter. Between God's art and man's there is a vast unbridgable chasm. Nature defies all imitation, but she invites interpretation, and most lovingly and generously rewards it. A clever painter knows that just as nature appeals *to the mind* through the eye, so must he appeal to it. It is common and significant enough to hear photographers in the presence of some great artistic camera picture asking its producer such questions as "What lens did you use for it?" "Who made the plate it was taken upon?" "What exposure did you give?" "How did you develop it?" and "Whose paper did you print upon?" All the enthusiasm of their admiration does not suffice to make them believe that its superior pictorial excellence and truthfulness are due to superior artistic knowledge, to accuracy of observation, judgment in selection, imagination, composition, feeling or sentiment. They never dream that it is superior because it is an intellectual product and not a mere mechanical production. They remind one of the old master-painter's scornful reply to the student who sounding aloud the praises of one of his pictures at last asked:—"What do you mix your colours with?" And was answered, "With brains, sir."

"The skill and craft of the artist will not be wasted if the vitality of truth, invoked by the power of genius and regulated by the judgment be wanted—all his work is then but so much wasted money, time, labour, skill and materials."* But mere miscroscopic sharpness in detail must not be regarded as truthfulness. If art was a mere question of realistic details, the photograph

---

* The Library of the Fine Arts (1831).

would be superior to the greatest painter's works, and a police reporter's record more powerfully truthful than a poet's drama.

In rigid cast-iron-looking landscapes we see but a sacrifice to outer accuracy and complete detail. The poetry of sunshine and air, the glories of space, the breathings of vitality and every retrospective and introspective suggestion of life, originality and emotion are all sacrificed for these inferior qualities. There are no resting-places for the birds in their black heavy foliage, no little cavernous recesses in which the flickering cast-shadows and merrily dancing sunshine are at play; solid-looking masses of black twigs, boughs and leaves seem as if not only the lightest breeze that blows, but the strongest blast would fail to make them rustle, quiver or bend, not a leaf seems movable, not a bough bendable. Looking at them one does not seem to hear the whispering air, or feel the glowing sunshine. In the fields they depict we do not sniff up perfumes of new-mown hay or in their gardens scent the flowers. They have on their seas and rivers not rising and falling, but risen or fallen waves petrified into stony immovability. Their shadows are flat dead surfaces with very little transparency and no reflected light or intermediate tones. They seem all alike, instead of being variably influenced by changeful conditions. And all this is not because the photographer's lens, plate and printing frame were utterly unsuited to the production of such things, but because the imagination of the operator never realized them, and he consequently never sought them. If he had more fully comprehended the meaning of truthfulness in art he would not have been so easily or so readily satisfied.

D

CHAPTER V.

ON THE EXPRESSION OF SPACE.

TURN we now from truthfulness generally to certain particular truths, beginning with that called space. To represent space (which means broadly air) truthfully is to do that which hitherto few, very few, photographers have done. It was one of the earliest difficulties to which artists called attention, and one which until quite recently photographers persistently overlooked or ignored.

I am taking no new ground, remember. In Sir William Newton's paper on " Art-photography," read in the year 1853, before the Society, he wrote (the italics were his own):—" Every variety of subject, from the most solid and substantial to the most light and airy, are displayed with that exactitude of delineation which completely sets at naught the exertions of *manual* ingenuity. Still the general tone of nature has yet to be accomplished by means of photography. Who has *not* studied nature so much as to observe how beautifully she throws her atmospheric veil, detaching each object, while producing that harmony and union of parts which the most splendid specimen of photography fails to realize. Consequently, *at present*, it is in vain to look for that true representation of light and shade in photography which is to be found in a fine work of art."

This means the truthful representation of atmosphere and perspective with which that of space is, of course, intimately associated.

Space may here be considered simply as space without going into all the more complicated considerations introduced by regarding it as air, with all its vast range of pictorial effects—sunlit, sunless, clear, misty, etc., etc. It is the business of an artistic landscape photographer to make that which really is a flat piece of paper look like space, to make objects that are round or square, deep or flat, seem so. Up to a certain point the expression of atmosphere and space are one, but the principles and rules of art blend so imperceptibly that in all these chapters we shall be continually approaching one subject from different points of view. Before dealing with aerial perspective in a separate chapter, let us therefore give some attention to the expressing of space.

If you wish to convey to the minds and imaginations of men true ideas of space, distant hills must not rise up before them with sharp, hard edges, nor must the nearest and most distant details be equally distinct, or as if they were so many flat, upright screens, set one behind another in the fashion of a set scene on the stage, instead of suggesting miles beyond miles of variegated scenery undergoing gradual changes as it retreats from the eye. To secure such effects in selecting time, place and hour, when exposing and when developing, and afterwards when regulating and controlling the printing, is a business of real importance, in pursuing which we can avail ourselves of those modifying and controlling influences which every experienced and accomplished artist-photographer now has at his finger ends. In the illustration on opposite page, everything in the composition aids in expressing space and atmosphere, the lines, the tones of dark and light, the harmonious blendings and the strong contrasts all serve to carry the eye as it were to the picture. It is a very suggestive little work well worth careful study.

First and foremost in importance let us give attention to what painters call " Values." If you examine a finished and carefully executed engraving from the work of some great landscape painter you will, if artistically observant, at once recognise the very colours of the original. This arises from the perfect union of two contrasting qualities, viz., tone and colour. All colours have their degrees of lightness or darkness (tones), and these degrees are continually changing with the changes

of air and illumination. In the grey of a dull day they are of course not what they are in sunshine. In pure daylight both the colours and their tones are most numerous, because it is white, and the tendency of all coloured light is to blend and render more or less imperceptible many gradations of colour-tones. Thus the rich orange of sunset illumination will convert what would be blue in white light into a warm grey, and pink and yellow light have a tendency to amalgamate the lighter tones, other colour-tones and hues assimilating or separating from the same causes in like way. If you want to study this for conviction, in a practical way, you may do so by ranging on a screen a diversity of colours with their tints and tones, throwing upon them differently-coloured lights and then photographing them.

The modern artist terms such effects " values," and the study he gives to them is usually thorough and careful. The photographer, as a rule, never gives them a thought. Their effects are particularly useful in expressing sentiment and feeling, and they are intimately allied with the study of cloud and sky effects. Of course, too, they play a most important part in expressing space.

Where the photographer finds this study more complicated than it is even to the painter is where the chemical action of colour has to be considered, and that concentrated intensity of colour for which the condensing power of his lens is responsible. These brilliant-coloured images although extremely beautiful on the focussing screen are very serious obstacles, although not generally recognised as such by photographic art-students. To render their works really truthful, however, these difficulties must be met and in one way or another conquered. Already photographic opticians, chemists, experimentalists and inventors, urged on by artist practitioners are on the scent, and within the last few years much has been done towards giving us means and materials wherewith to combat such difficulties. Colour screens and the orthochromatic process are perhaps of these the most important.

A very clever landscape painter once assured us that he never truly understood the real meanings of colour until a commission for a large number of monochrome pictures taught him the importance of their tones in suggesting colour to the imagination and in expressing the varying conditions of space and atmosphere. In the

Art Student for July, 1864, we have the remarks of yet another painter* who said :—" Working all along with colours I fancied I had achieved a thorough mastery of them in their various qualities, modifications and combinations, but I never dreamt of studying the monotones of colours separately, never recognised the necessity of such effort to acquire any proper understanding of colour. Consequently when I began to paint with brown and white only, I was like a lame man deprived of his crutches."

This relationship of tones and colours being largely influenced by atmospheric causes, have consequently a very important bearing on expressing space, and should therefore receive careful attention in the practice of landscape photography for the production of pictures. There are also other ways in which the due expression of space is often missed, and on which passing comment may here be appropriately made. To some of these we must next give attention.

The cast shadows of sunlight are beautifully transparent, delicate and tender, although very clearly defined. Under-exposed or not properly developed in a negative they become hard, opaque and too coarsely and severely outlined. Their natural beauty and softness thus lost arises from the presence of strongly reflected lights and constantly differing thicknesses of atmosphere. If these subtle and varied effects are not secured by exposure, development and artistic printing, we have misrepresentation not only of tones or values, and of colours as indicated by their tones, but also of space. For twenty or more years we are told that the greatest colourist of our generation, Turner, could not " colour," and never would be a colourist because he had " no eye for colour."

* Who in 1870 became a clever photographer.

Why? The cause was his not having then studied colours in their tones. The paintings he made during these years were mostly in water-colours and after the fashion of the old school of water-colour painters, were drawn and painted from nature in sepia or Indian ink before the colours were added in flat washes, and often in the studio. The effect he thus obtained was rather that of a coloured print or photograph than what we now recognise as a finished water-colour picture. But it always seemed to me that this was a kind of apprenticeship period, and that his experience with gradations of monochrome was the real basis of his glorious after-triumphs in colour, and in *the expressing, with such wonderful force, air and space.* It taught him the importance of tones, or what we now call values. What Turner learned in this way is just what the photographer who desires to excel in landscape art must also learn.

Turn to the works of another great landscape painter, Claude, and you will see how he too studied values. Go to the National Gallery in London, and look at his little wafer of time-discoloured once white oil paint, which even at its purest and newest was black in comparison with the dazzling brilliancy of the sun it represents. See how this absurdly dingy little hieroglyph floods the painted landscape with its glory. This grand result is not due to the painted sun, and only in part to the colour. It owes nearly all its power to Claude's knowledge and uses of tones and their values. Throughout all nature, in every changeful season of the year, in every variation from the brightness of early dawn, until twilight's dim obscurity, the tones and expressions of a landscape are continually altering, and every alteration is a new study for the artist, a new glory for the imaginative, each having its own associated ideas and suggestions.

THE EXPRESSION OF SPACE. 57

Example.—Illustrating the Effect of Curved Lines running into a Picture. From a Photograph by J. P. Gibson.

THE EXPRESSION OF SPACE.   59

Another element whereby space is expressed in a picture is linear perspective. "Lines," says Henry Howard, R.A., "link the parts together and lead the eye agreeably through the picture. They form the melody of the work, and in all compositions should arise out of the particular occasion, should be flowing and graceful, or more direct and abrupt, as may suit the character of the subject." The quality they thus realize is intimately connected with the expressing of space, and this is

Example—Expression of Lines.

greatly aided by the fact that all straight lines given by retiring surfaces run to what draughtsmen call vanishing points, the position of which indicates the height and position of the lens or the eye of some human spectator. But this will, if space permits, be more fully and practically dealt with in the following chapter. It is mentioned here only to show its connection with the expression of space with which lines are very intimately connected. Every line carries the eye of the spectator into the picture, or away from it, consequently while playing an important part in pictorial composition, and adding to general truthfulness of effect. The illustration on page 59 will show my meaning. It is a bit of old Venice, and the perspective lines of the architecture at once seize the eye of the spectator and convey the perception of space with great force.

Foregrounds and figures properly introduced and selected are also very influential elements in expressing space, but these I must deal with presently for they are important enough to have an entire chapter to themselves.

It should also be borne in mind that in expressing space we secure relief in all its varying degrees, bringing this forward, throwing that back—making one feature dominant, another subordinate, and so on, according to the requirements of pictorial composition, or the artist's dominant purpose. But this power comes, as we have already asserted, from culture not from chance, from intellectual effort not from mere mechanical practice.

CHAPTER VI.

ON SKIES, CLOUDS, AERIAL PERSPECTIVE AND ATMOSPHERIC EFFECTS.

WE have already pointed out, or suggested, that every hour of the day has its characteristic atmospheric and pictorial effects. The air in the sky above and on the earth beneath is a grand source of pictorial beauty. With what eloquence John Ruskin describes the sky as "that part of creation in which Nature has done more for the sake of pleasing man, more for the sole and evident purpose of talking to him and teaching him, than in any other of her works. . . . There is not," he adds, "a moment of any day in our lives when nature is not producing scene after scene, picture after picture, glory after glory, and working still upon such exquisite and constant principles of the most perfect beauty in that glorious dome, for the good and delight of all the dwellers on earth. It is the realm of beauty, beauty raised to the loftiest in order that all may see."

Its changes are often so subtle, and the differences come and go so gradually, with such seemingly eccentric blendings and dissolutions that only the watchful detect them. Even the slightest changes in these atmospherical conditions are often of the greatest importance from a pictorial point of view. Just as distance sometimes makes harsh, loud noises soft and musical, so the partial thickening of air, or some chance mistiness, such as we often note veiling masses of dark shadow under leafy trees at certain hours, will change masses of dark shadow in Nature into opaque flat chemically blackened paper breaking up the harmony of "values" and destroying the effect of space and distance. In like way a grassy field which photographs too uniformly dark, rising up like a screen instead of retiring flatly, will if taken when the dew is on it produce a far more satisfactory result, the silvery greyness of the moisture being more actinic than the rich full green. Again, to get the flashing effect of sunlight on the burnished surfaces of lakes or rivers, is a photographic difficulty often encountered and seldom conquered. But select a spot where you see water weed of a greenish grey colour abounding—as it often does—and that difficulty is generally overcome. In like way the delicate pink blush and pale green sometimes seen in the sky at sunset has helped many a thoughtfully observant photographer in securing in its full beauty a pictorial sky-effect which might otherwise have been lost through over-exposure. Colour steals into air and dissolves out of it with imperceptible gradations, and like other desirable aerial effects must be watched and waited for. So every landscape should be photographed or painted with the knowledge that each scene in Nature varies in aspect as the cloudland above it does. Here is a picture from Dante (Carey's translation) which is in the same way suggestive.

> Call to remembrance, reader, if thou e'er
> Hast on a mountain top, been ta'en by cloud,
> Through which thou sawest no better than the mole
> Doth through opaceous membrane; then, whene'er
> The watery vapours began to melt
> Into thin air, how faintly the sun's sphere
> Seemed wading through them.

"The level marshes and rich meadows of the tertiary, the rounded swells and short pastures of the chalk, the square-built cliffs and cloven dells of the lower limestone, the soaring peaks and ridgy precipices of the primaries, have nothing in common among them, nothing which is not distinctive and incommunicable," says Ruskin. And this is peculiarly true of atmospheric effects belonging to them. "Their clouds are different," he goes on, "their humours of storm and sunshine are different." In every work of art that is loftily true to its noblest mission, the grandeur and power of the result is "proportioned to the unity of feeling manifested in its several parts." And clouds, as an old number of Black-

Sky and Water Effect with Figures.

wood says, "Clouds are to the heavens what human beings are to the earth," and they really are as important and useful in the stories they tell as human beings are in landscapes.

The other day I was reading in a photographic journal a well-written, otherwise thoughtful paper, in which the writer advised his brothers of the camera to shirk certain difficulties by confining their picture-making efforts to scenes without any wide expanses of distant country. What gems of pictorial effect, what charms of sunny atmosphere and floating cloud shadows, what opportunities of catching the rarer beauties of Nature would be lost to photography if such advice were generally adopted ! What compensation would it be to have sharply defined forms and perfect details when we had sacrified that expression of space, and that atmosphere and sky which, as Ruskin said, is "sometimes gentle, sometimes capricious, sometimes awful; almost human in its passions, almost spiritual in its tenderness, almost divine in its infinity, surely meant for the chief teacher of what is immortal in us." "And, although," as he adds, "we never attend to it, never make it a subject of thought, but as it has to do with our animal sensations."

Describing how certain great masters of landscape painted air and light, he says David Cox gave us "dew-laden air" and "soft white clouds melting with their own motion"; that Copley Fielding, "casting his whole soul into space," mingled "light and vapour," "always with a passion for Nature's freedom burning in his heart"; that J. D. Harding delighted in revelations of "Nature's own sunshine"; following it "into the crannies of the rocks and along the flanks of the sloping hills"; and that Clarkson Stanfield, "concealing nothing and falsifying nothing," modelled "the masses of the clouds with the strength of tempest in their every fold"; and Turner painted "with the elements waiting upon his will, and the night and morning obedient to his call."

And again, when describing Turner's grand picture of Venice, he dwells upon the way in which that wonderful painter reveals a "white flashing fulness of dazzling light which the waves drink and the clouds breathe, bending and burning in intensity of joy." He says of its sky, "it is visible infinity, liquid, measureless, unfathomable, panting and melting through the chasms in the long fields of snow-white, flaked, slow-moving vapours, down to the islanded rest of the Enganean hills." Comparing this dream of Venice glorified by sunshine and air to the wonderfully photographic-like picture which lens-aided Canaletti painted of the same subject, he says of the latter, it is Venice as she was seen " by the most unfeeling and untaught of mankind. The bargeman and bricklayer probably see no more in Venice than Canaletti gives. . . . . What more there is in Venice than brick and stone — what there is of mystery and death and memory and beauty, what there is to be learned or lamented, to be loved or wept over, we look for to Canaletti in vain." To all intents and purposes Canaletti painted what the lens saw, not what he saw, for he used a camera and painted from its transparent screen.

Of Stanfield's Venetian painting he complains in a like spirit, despite its acknowledged merits. " Beautiful as it is, it lacks poetical associations, feeling and sentiment." And yet how vastly superior to the best photograph of Venice I have come across (the best by-the-bye I saw in Naples) is Stanfield's splendid picture. But in even this admirable Neapolitan photograph the sky selected was one in which nothing was suggested more than it actually represented a literal fact, a kind of empty box fact, something with nothing in it.

Atmospherical perspective is associated with tones just as linear perspective belongs to forms, and each is equally essential to truthful representation. " It not only embraces," says Barnard, " all the numerous effects of atmosphere denominated by artists the keeping of a picture, but it is of the greatest importance in all contrasts or oppositions of light and shade.* It is therefore

* See also Chapter XII. on Breadth.

highly desirable that the student should be directed to the examination and here again careful comparison of your production with Nature is needed." . . . " In the foreground of a picture the colours " (in our case their tones) " may be supposed to have their true force, the lights in this part being brightest and the shadows darkest. The distance of a hundred yards may be represented by one veil, a mile by a second, four miles by a third, and the extreme distance by a fourth. . . . . When by such experiments combined with the study of real effects in the open air the student becomes aware how indispensable it is to represent atmosphere, he will never rest satisfied until he can imitate the effect in his pictures " whether they be paintings of photographs.

" We destroy," says Ruskin (I can give you on this subject no words so clear and forcible, no authority more weighty), " we destroy," says he, " both space and size " (proportion) " either by the vacancy which affords us no measure of space, or the distinctness which gives us a false one."

Atmosphere in shadow and atmosphere in light contrast each other very powerfully, and with such wonderful diversities of pictorial effect that only a watchfully observant eye will recognise them either in nature or on the focussing screen, and he who does not grasp such creations in his mind is not likely to time exposure and delicately manipulate development with a view to their representation. How rare, for instance, it is to find in landscape photography that faint misty effect of air in strong sunshine which makes objects seen through it appear as if delicately and beautifully veiled, while other objects on the same plane being less strongly affected, are so distinct that you may trace even their smaller details.

SKIES, CLOUDS, AERIAL PERSPECTIVE, ETC. 67

"The appearance of mist, or whiteness in the blue of the sky," says Ruskin, "is a circumstance which, more or less, accompanies sunshine, and which, supposing the quantity of vapour constant, is greatest in the brightest sunlight." When there are no clouds in the sky the whiteness affects the whole sky equally. But when there are clouds between us and the sun, and the sun is low, these clouds cast shadows along and through the mass of suspended vapour with striking effect.

Composition of Shipping and Figures.

Within the shadows, the vapour being transparent and invisible, the sky appears of a pale blue. But where the sunbeams strike the vapour, they become visible in the form of beams, radiating shafts of light which are most valuable pictorially, and the constant accompaniments of a low sun. The denser the mist the more distinct and sharp-edged will these rays be. When the air is very clear they are vague, " flushing, graduated passages of light "; when the air is very thick they are " keen-edged and decisive in a very high degree."

It is in this direction of atmospheric effect that artist photographers will encounter at once their most glorious opportunities and their most perplexing difficulties, but I see no reason on earth why they should be despairingly rejected as things impossible of attainment so long as photographic art remains as vigorously and hopefully progressive as it now is.

Photographic landscapes are commonly wanting most in those passages wherein the objects become lost by softly melting away from sight into air, the result being nigh akin to that hard, map-like flattening out of natural objects, which is in most instances due rather to the producer's want of observation and artistic taste than to the unavoidable restrictions of the chemico-optical process and tools. Once more, I purposely repeat, once more do not suppose that picturesque treatment means violence done to the truthfulness of photography; quite the contrary, its truthfulness is increased in proportion with its pictorial merit. All improvements of this kind merely obey those necessary principles by which both art and nature make assemblages of numerous and varied objects so agreeable to the eye. And although this due balance of part with part is largely the result of what we call linear perspective, by which the quality of the lens and the ability of its user are equally tested, they are still more largely the result of that which is more difficult to secure, aerial perspective. Without truthfulness in atmospheric representation, mere linear perspective, dealing with relative magnitudes and shapes, becomes itself imperfect and misleading. Distance by diminishing the size of this or that object, gives no clue to its absolute size or comparative magnitude; aerial effects, however, suggest at once not only how far or how near they are, but the extent to which they are influenced by various conditions of light, etc.

A photo-picture without atmospherical perspective and its subordinating effects resembles a mere jumble of meaningless words, confusing both mind and eye.

Leslie, the painter, used to say there was no high-minded ambitious work done by the pseudo student, unless it taught him to see better what he copied; in other words, mere hand-work without head-work is sure to be degenerate and uninteresting. In nothing is this more clearly seen than it is in landscape photographs. Atmosphere is the great harmonizing element of a picture, the chief element of beauty, it is the eye's music*, giving order and proportion with the pervading tone, high or low, and consequently the pervading sentiment or feeling. A rich effect or a simple one may be made to prevail by its judicious introduction, selection or treatment. Without atmospheric peculiarities or characteristics every landscape picture is flat, monotonous and uninteresting. The photographer who goes to the study of nature as an artist or poet does, reverently, with trained perceptive organs, will find the pleasure and delight of his work largely increased. Sturm wrote well and truly when he said, "The advantages of reason are never more felt than when our faculties are employed in meditating upon the perfection of God displayed in His works."

Many of the old landscape painters show us how little study of this kind existed amongst them; but modern painters have of late been feeling alive to its importance, and by comparing the former with the latter, camera artists may learn useful lessons. In the former's works, the distance used to be always coldly blue and the foregrounds invariably aglow with rich warm colour whatever the hour of the day, time of year or proper

* This word is used to indicate the appropriateness in proportion, size and tones which is consistent with the natural union of parts to make the whole at once attractive and beautiful.

condition of atmosphere. Obviously this was false and inartistic.

Not less untruthful are photographers who in a like way misrepresent the tones which belong to *colours*, so that foreground, middle, and extreme distance are either too violent in their changes or jumbled all together, and look like flat screens placed one behind another, rather than gradually retiring surfaces.

I know only too well what difficulties there are in realizing all a thoughtful, observant and imaginative artist sees in nature, by chemical and optical appliances. But I also know that these difficulties are not less to the painter and that they have from time to time, in various ways, been more or less triumphantly overcome by photographers. Anything which has been done demonstrates that it can be done. Not by foolish, ill-disguised trickery and deception, as so many suggest, but by thoroughly legitimate, honest, valorous art work.

The greater the power you have in modifying and altering, the greater necessity there is for obtaining the knowledge which gives that power its real value. To increase artistic possibilities, operators, opticians and chemists have of late, as our photographic journals clearly show, been inventing new and valuable appliances, but the better the tools the greater the cleverness of the tool-user should be ; otherwise they are uselsss, perhaps worse than useless. A blunt knife is safer than a sharp knife in the hands of one who uses it awkwardly. Clouds, for instance, which are the results of a little wool and a masking dodge in the printing are, in this way, often better than others printed from the most beautiful cloud negatives. The photographer who prints in a cloudy sky taken at noon, above a quiet landscape taken in the morning or evening, commits blunders which are only the worse for being separately perfectly natural and truthful. We see every month in our society meetings, specimens in which such self-evident necessities of artistic work are ignorantly, culpably or carelessly overlooked. One would think, that the producers of these landscape photographs and "cloud negatives" regarded the sky as something altogether unreal and unimportant; as if clouds indicated by their shapes, densities, heights, modelling, light and shade, nothing that had any real meaning. To them they probably have not. They go to work as if clouds never intercepted light, and never cast shadows, never appealed to us in inexhaustible sentiments of beauty and grandeur; never even indicated or governed those rare or common atmospherical conditions which give every real picture its dominant merit. I have seen photographs with clouds low above still water in which they had no reflections, and over which they cast no shadows. I have seen really perfect cloud negatives made utterly untruthful by mere overprinting, in a way that could never have satisfied the operator if he had been observant of nature or the possessor of artistic knowledge.

Clouds associating themselves with their true meanings in a work of art assume certain distinctive forms. These are so well known to ordinary well-informed folk that there are distinctive names for them, as stratus, nimbus, linear-cirrus, cumoid-cirrus, cumlo-stratus, cumulus, or mottled cirro-stratus, etc., each of these names expressing conditions by which not only the clouds but the entire landscape must be affected. How often in sky and landscape photographs we see these facts overlooked.

Clouds are however, almost infinite in their variety of forms, although they are for practical purposes thus broadly classified and distinguished. Sometimes as cirrus they appear filmy and transparent as veils of barely perceptible silver threads; or as dark, solid-looking, heavy masses of cumulus, hanging low and near the earth, when the atmosphere is damp and thick; sometimes swept into long parallel streaks by coming storm wind, sometimes piled up in mountainous forms, or spreading over the entire sky like a grey curtain. But they are always eloquent in expression and meaning; always in their silent languages they tell us forcibly their various influences, all more or less important for our story-telling purposes. To use them in separate negatives without regard to their utterances or to so associate their utterances that they flatly contradict one another, is so palpably, so absurdly wrong, that there should be no need to say a word about them, and yet the need of saying something does exist, or this book of mine would never have been written.

Another objection to the thoughtless use of cloud negatives is in the fact that the photographer commonly forgets that when motion is caught (and it is a fruitful source of the pictorial in art) the forms given by it often indicate that point from which the wind blows. If the trees and grasses, weeds and rushes of the landscape indicate by their curves wind from the west, and the clouds say it is from the east, artists will smile and the unkind will jeer at the artistic pretensions of photographers generally. Or, if the wind is in the air just above the landscape, and none in the air below, the blunder will be not less conspicuous. If again, the mournful and solemn gloom of the sky is contrasted by bright sunny effects in the cheerful landscape—and even this I have seen in more than one photographic exhibition—the error, you would fancy, should be sufficiently obvious. Yet it has escaped observation and even been defended when pointed out, on the ground that it was artistic to study brilliant effects of light and shade without regard to commonplace, ordinary facts. But how can this accord with the productions of an art the highest and most valued quality of which has from the first been its claim to truthfulness?

A well known landscape painter, J. Barnard, whom I have already quoted, says: "All opportunities of studying the phenomena of nature should be embraced." As a general rule in landscapes the hour of the day should be evident. To assist in showing this, we must summon to our aid a knowledge of the different conformation of clouds, as displayed at various periods of the day. Thus morning, either before or after sunrise, will be indicated as much by the form of the clouds as by their colours, or, if cloudless, by the appearance of the dawn in the sky, by the summit of the hills alone being touched with light, or by mists lying in the valley; mid-day by the direction of the shadows, reflections, or general expressions of heat, calmness, and repose. In the evening an exact chronometer is afforded by the height of the sun above the horizon.

However the sky-effect may be produced, it should be in accordance with the landscape's character and its most strongly prevailing sentiment or feeling, otherwise it will destroy the ideas it should create, and weaken where it should strengthen.

Calm, peaceful sky-effects blend most harmoniously with landscape views of a quiet, pastoral description. Sky and landscape necessarily associating themselves in nature should therefore do so in a photograph. Underprinting a sky negative frequently spoils the general effect, and this is yet another reason why the photographer should be a close observer of nature, comparing what he sees with what he produces just as carefully and conscientiously as if he were wielding pencil and brush instead of lens and camera. It is excellent practice to get a print from your negative, and taking it to the scene it was taken from, carefully compare the two, noting especially the tones and values of sky and landscape as expressing aerial effect in the landscape below and the sky above. In many cases I am sure the photographer who did this would go back and print from or develop his next negative with new and valuable ideas.

The photographer who does nothing of the kind, but relies entirely upon apparatus, materials and strict observance of certain mechanical practices, finds commonplace ordinary scenes and effects quite good enough for him. He does not miss air or space. If the middle distance comes out more clear and distinct than the near foreground, he does not see why one object should modestly retire which staringly advances, or why one which retires ought to advance, or if they do one or the other he does not understand what he had or could have had to do with it. His lens is excellent; if the picture it gives is untrue, the optician is the culprit, if there is a culprit, but says he "that can't be." If his photographs do not give light and shade accurately, the faults must be, he imagines, in the preparation of his plates, but "that also is impossible, for he bought them ready for use of the best maker in the market." For anything wrong, it is always the tools that are blamable. But of every success the credit is entirely his own. He has no real ambition, no artistic aspirations, or he overestimates a superficial acquaintance with art, thinking—

"The soundest judge of merit known
Is he who justly estimates his own."

Take an engraving of Turner's "Venice," and you will recognise in it the air and sunlight of which Ruskin speaks so enthusiastically. Shut out the sky and you will still see sunshine, filling "the blue sea between us with the fulness of its wings," and troubling "the shadows of those azure, fathomless depths of crystal mystery, on which the swiftness of the poised gondola floats double" by "the quivering of its bright reflections." In it we perceive, if the engraving is a good one, as in the painting, "dream-like and dim, but glorious, unnumbered palaces lifting their shafts out of the hollow sea—pale ranks of motionless flame—their mighty towers sent up to heaven like tongues of more eager fire, their grey domes looming out vast and dark like eclipsed worlds, their sculptured arabesques and purple marbles fading further and fainter, league beyond league, lost in the *light* of distance." I have italicised the word "light," for objects die away and fade in a full noon-tide blaze of vaporous sunlight, as often as they do into the misty gloom of sunset. Tones may range from pensive and solemn to light and cheerful, through long passages of pearly gradations, subtle in delicacy and tenderness, and through combinations of strong, rich full dark gradations, but they always suggest colours under certain conditions of light and air. Some are allied to passages of the utmost brilliancy and intensity, stealing out of and melting into it almost imperceptibly. Others take short, swift, rapid strokes into or out of sunshine, into or out of profound gloom. And sometimes a single landscape combines both these conditions in picturesque and striking contrast, but they are always controlled by cloud and sky, light and air. A dark cloud scudding across a summer sky will give us such effects on distant hill sides, or ranges of woody mountains, or along a wide expanse of lake or shoreless ocean, and very beautiful they are. Gay, sad, solemn, or picturesque, brilliantly forcible or modestly subordinate, these tones are all alike governed by the dominating influences of the ever-changing atmosphere.

I have in my eye just now the shop-windows of two photographers. In one I see the most mechanically photographic of photographs. They have no natural gradation of tones, no real separations of distances, nothing to suggest atmosphere or the assimilating or dominating character of the light by which they were " taken "—no beauty of thought or feeling. Distinctness of detail and uniformity of general effect without any other idea pervades them in every part. The focusser evidently strove to secure an equality of " sharpness " as the loftiest aim of his art. The developer strove to intensify his high-lights and preserve his shadows transparent, destroying depth, space and perspective, to get surface effects only, ignoring the most delicate as well as the strongest tones with all their subtle intermediates, exposing and developing without a thought beyond, over or under printing, mechanically and uniformly, without giving the slightest connection to the accurate representation of atmosphere or light. The spaces where skies should have been are nothing but flat, meaningless patches of grey and white, or bare blank spaces of pure white paper.

In the other photographer's windows most of the pictures are from the same subjects, yet how different! Life, light, space and motion are seen in them. The skies are real skies, changes wrought by atmosphere are all more or less faithfully indicated, everything is not equally strong in detail, the gradations are not almost everywhere alike. It seems to me that here is the work of one who saw his subject at various times and under differing conditions, studied it before he chose it, and then exposed his plate with a clear conception of what he wanted. He probably took two negatives in rapid succession, one of the winding river, church and trees, with distant hills, and another of the sky, because the light on clouds, their grouping and cast shadows are all in harmonious accord with the lights, shadows and atmospheric effects in the landscape beneath them. The clouds have solidity and variety of forms and differing densities, suggesting air instead of accidentally stained paper. They receive light and throw shadows in proportion to their position and densities, they are near and distant, they belong to both earth below and sky above. Colour is suggested in the tones of these productions, as motion, sunlight, heat and wind are. We see the wind in the rushes, depth in the water, space in the atmosphere, birds in the trees, human pleasure and peaceful enjoyment, a spot to rest in, a spot to fish in, a spot to go a-dreaming in—in short, a picture as well as a photograph. And all these things come from faithfully representing sunlight and air, in other words, from that sky which, as Ruskin says, " we never make the subject of a thought but as it has to do with our animal sensations, but look upon all which bears witness to the intention of the Supreme that we are to receive more from the covering vault than the light and dew which we share with the weed and the worm, but as a succession of meaningless or monotonous accidents too common and too vain to be worthy of a moment of watchfulness or a glance of admiration." As he says: " Who among the whole chattering crowd can tell of the forms and the precipices of the chain of tall white mountains that girded the horizon at noon yesterday ? Who saw the narrow sunbeam that came out of the south and smote upon their summits until they melted and mouldered away in a dust of blue rain ? Who saw the dance of the dead clouds when the sunlight left them last night and the west wind blew them before it like withered leaves ?" I wish one could truthfully say that many photographers have seen and recorded these glorious sky pictures, catching their meanings and bringing to their expression in art, every power that its language commands. But I think we can truthfully say that of late years quite enough has been seen in the way of cloud and sky-photographs to inspire their producers with faith in the artistic future of their art.

The vapour and sunshine effects already alluded to as giving those great fan-like "radiating shafts of light" are those which test not only the photographer's technical and artistic knowledge but his manipulative dexterity also, being often so exceedingly subtle and delicate as to be easily destroyed in the processes of exposing, developing and printing.

And this brings to mind a photograph I once exhibited and commented upon to illustrate a paper which I read before the South London Society of many years ago. It was a large and wonderfully beautiful photograph, but while its sky gave us these radiating rays at their sharpest and brightest, indicating a dense quantity of vapour in the atmosphere, the distant hills of the landscape associated with it showed that it was taken when the sun was high, and the atmosphere exceptionally free from mist or vapour of any kind. No one who had studied nature and knew anything of aerial effects could have perpetrated such a blunder, yet not one of the half a hundred or so of photographers present detected the blunder before I pointed it out, and received for so doing neither thanks nor compliments. Our president (a scientific man of some rank, and a clergyman whom we all very truly loved and respected) said in the kindest way possible that such a mistake, if a mistake it might be called, was a mere spot on the sun which only increased the beauty and interest of such a very charming production, a sentiment which was received with applause. I endured the reproof patiently enough, although it was certainly discouraging, and not being "convinced against my will" was "of the same opinion still." Mr. Hammerton, in his "Life of Turner," speaking of that artist's famous picture of Kilchurn Castle, painted in 1801, remarked:—"I know the topography of the place quite thoroughly, with that minuteness which is only possible to a resident who takes the keenest interest in the neighbourhood where he lives and makes landscape painting his main occupation." And then he pointed out that Turner's point of view was one at which the castle he represented must have been invisible; that he put sailing boats where, because of the violent gusts of wind commonly encountered, no sails could have been used, because he wanted something to cut the base line of his mountain, and so throw the mountain further back. He made the castle, not the picturesque ruin overgrown with ivy it really is, but, for some unaccountable reason, a clumsy, ugly, square block of masonry unbroken by anything in the way of vegetable growth. He represented a peakless mountain sloping upward gradually by one rising abruptly to a peak at a height enormously greater. The falsehood was unnecessary, and the picture would have been better if it had been truthful; still it is a picture of remarkable power and beauty, and moreover one in which the sky effect gives these radiating lines of light, and this vaporous atmosphere of which I have spoken. But the air through which we see the wild rugged mountain and grim old fortress, the lake, the low-lying clouds, cliffs, hills and boats, is one and the same all over the picture. Turner never perpetrated such a blunder as that which was pointed out to the South Londoners. His untruths were told of the least, not the most important aspects of Nature.

"The real motive of Turner's picture," says Hammerton, " was not Kilchurn, but the play of clouds about the crest of a Highland mountain—which mountain signified little. The mountain is any mountain you please, the castle is any castle you please. The clouds play about the granite peak, a shower falling here from their trailing fringes, a sunbeam flashing there on the toppling silvery billows which are their ever-changing summits, a level wreath of white vapour clinging in the shelter of the peak itself, great volumes rolling and surging in the abyss of the deep corrie, and on the steep stony sides of the mountains the purple shadows fall vast and swift, veiling each of them its hundred acres of desolation. Who thinks of man's works when he witnesses the majesty of the storms on the everlasting mountains?" Still the fact remains, Turner called his picture what it was not, and however grand his triumph and however true his dealings with air and sunshine his art was to that extent untruthful. I have quoted our best art critics to have their authority on my side and thus win your confidence. But it must be borne in mind that they speak of painting only. Thus in all his suggestions, Ruskin has colour in view, and some one may urge that what he advocates is therefore altogether beyond the photographer's reach. But those who make such objection overlook a fact I have already mentioned. If the photograph does not give colour it suggests it, for every colour has its tone. Critics of works in black and white know this so well that they use and rightly use the word "colour" to indicate combinations of tones; one monochrome picture they tell us is "full of *colour*," and of another they say "there is no *colour* in it," meaning that the tones do or do not convey to our mind's eye the colours of Nature.

A very old acquaintance and fellow-worker of mine, Valentine Blanchard, pointed out in *The Practical Photographer* of July, 1892, other blunders made in producing skies inartistically. He said, "frequently the camera is pointed upward in working for the cloud negatives, probably to avoid some tree, or house, or telegraph post, and in consequence the clouds too nearly overhead are taken, and these same clouds are printed into extensive landscapes," (with of course quite another horizon line) " and thus, instead of a glorious perspective of clouds gradually receding, until in the extreme distance they lose form and melt away, a mass of clouds appears far too large for the subject, and too strongly defined, and, therefore, completely wanting in aerial perspective. If the camera is in a horizontal position when the scene is taken, and is afterwards pointed up at an angle of forty-five degrees to take the clouds, what can result but such an abnormal effect as I have described." I shall conclude this chapter with another quotation from the same practical authority. When dealing with controversial matters one likes to be well supported.

"Whenever possible—that is to say, whenever there are clouds suitable to the subject—it is well to take two negatives, one of the landscape and one of the clouds. In the first the full exposure, so as to secure proper detail in foreground, should be given ; whilst in the second the most rapid of snap-shots will be sufficient to secure detail in even the most delicate clouds. When the latter negative is developed of course a proper combination of these two negatives will produce a perfectly harmonious result, particularly if the right effect has been patiently waited for. It sometimes happens that the combination of cloud and landscape is most striking; in such a case blaze away with all the enthusiasm that such a subject demands, but as a rule the patient worker is the one who gets the greatest reward for his labour."

I will also venture to extract from *The Practical Photographer*, of July 1st, 1894, some very sound practical

F

hints by another widely recognised authority, who says :—

"The artist tones down and harmonizes what are really violent contrasts, when measured by volumes of light; while the sensitive film has no such selective power, but must receive the varying volumes of light in their full intensity, so that when the initial action of the light (termed by photographers, exposure) is completed by the developer, the result is in such cases above referred to, violent contrast, leaving an impression on the mind quite opposed to that which it received from the view itself, where all was harmony."

"The kind of views admittedly which photography does most justice to are seascapes and sky effects where there is but little contrast, and where, owing to the volume of light, motion and life can be obtained with rapid exposures. The question, then, for consideration is, can we by any known process modify either the exposure or the development, so as to bring about the desired harmony, or can it be obtained in any other way? Some skilled photographers recommend that two negatives should be taken of every strongly contrasted view, the one to be exposed for the foreground and shadow, the other for the distance and sky, presumably the middle distance can be printed from whichever of the two best harmonizes. Of course, making two negatives means loss of time and extra trouble, but to the earnest photographer this should not prove a hindrance. The second mode of remedying the defect is in the development. The writer well remembers reading some years since a paper by Captain Abney describing how he developed an Alpine scene, in which figures and shadows were in the foreground, and snow-peaked mountains in the distance. The *modus operandi*—writing from memory —consisted of exposing for the foreground, thereby greatly over-exposing for the distance ; afterwards modifying the development by using a minimum of pyro, until all the detail was out, and then bringing up the density by further addition of pyro. The writer can only remark on this, that if such be practicable, then the wonder is that so few follow on the lines given, and that so many harshly black and white productions are to be seen."

"The third means of obtaining harmony is one that perhaps but few photographers have given any thought to, but to the writer it appears a possible one, that is, by investing the camera itself with a certain amount of selective power. Clearly such is not possible with the ordinary camera, where the entire view is made at one operation, and all parts receive practically the same exposure. But accepting the eye as our guide, let us suppose that a photograph can be taken with a revolving camera, the light acting on the sensitive film through a narrow vertical slit ; then we should have an approximation to the action of the eye, and a certain selective power in the apparatus, not nearly to the same extent as in ordinary vision, where the image is built up, spot by spot, but still far more than we have at present. The image would be formed line by line, and it would be in the power of the operator, not to open or close the diaphragm, but to alter the duration of the exposure, and so bring about a similar result."

Another excellent practical suggestion which could be utilised effectually in seeking passing brilliant sky and cloud effects was made in *The Practical Photographer* for July, 1895. It was that of a camera in which the simultaneous action of twin lenses would enable the operator to watch the image on his focussing screen and make the exposure, without the slightest delay, directly the effect he desired to secure appeared. For as the writer says many beautiful pictures are lost and many plates spoiled by the few seconds delay caused by removing the focussing glass and putting the dark slide in its place. In the same article the writer (Mr. Harold Baker) gives another admirable hint which, as it has also a practical bearing on this subject, I repeat. It was originally given by Captain Abney who tells us that a lens exposed to a bright light for some minutes while the focussing is going on, absorbs sufficient of the light to produce a kind of phosphoresence sufficient to fog an extremely sensitive plate. By focussing with one lens and exposing with another this very possible danger would be escaped. But to return to Nature and artistic selection. The power which strong sunlight has of blotting out detail and softening and blending relative parts should be looked for and studied with a view to reproduction in the camera and negative. This power is sometimes very curiously exercised; for instance, cast shadows which in half-light are strongly marked are sometimes in very brilliantly lighted passages of the middle distance quite extinguished; moreover they are sometimes traceable on the focussing screen when they are quite unseen by the human eye. This should be borne in mind.

Again, partial hazy atmospheric effects, and effects of vapour, rain and mist, are often most picturesque and poetically suggestive in a landscape, although few photographers dare encounter the technical difficulties they present. Some of the most charming landscape paintings I can remember represented misty evening effects, when the light was low, and ghostly grey veils floating upwards from river and valley assumed strange mystically suggestive images. And some photographers I have seen followed closely in their wake and got quite marvellous examples of what may be accomplished pictorially by the proper choice and management of a lens, the time of exposure, the method of development and certain dexterous schemes for regulating and controlling development and printing. P. G. Hammerton, comparing one of Gustave le Grey's marine photographs with Holman Hunt's lovely little picture called " Fairlight Downs—Sunlight on the Sea," says, "the blaze of light upon the sea is given in the photograph with perfect fidelity; but in order to get this and the light on the edges of the clouds all else has been sacrificed; the shaded sides of the clouds, in nature of a dazzling grey, brighter than white paper, are positively black in the photograph, and the pale splendour of the sunlit sea, except where it *flashes* light, is heavy and impenetrable darkness. Towards the sides of the photograph the distinction between sea and sky is wholly lost in one uniform shade of dark-brown, extending from top to bottom without any indication of a horizon. . . . . The crowning falsity is the sun itself, which is *darker* than the surrounding clouds, being simply a grey wafer on a white ground." Turning from the photographer's to the painter's work, he speaks of "the sunlight itself, in its broad, white glare on the water under the sun, and its gradual scattering into glitter to the right hand and the left; in its long lines in the distance, divided by the shadows of clouds; in its restless flashings on the crests of the little waves far away, it is as true, or truer, than the photograph; but here all comparison ends, because there is no longer in the photograph anything to be compared with the picture. Where the photograph is simply dark-brown, the picture is full of the most delicate gradations and the sweetest play of tone. Where the glitter is not, we have still the sunlit beauty of the fair sea, which is indeed better and more precious even than the glitter itself, just as the fairness of a beautiful woman is better than the glitter and flash of her diamonds.

And there is a hot haze in the blending distance miles away, and there is a sultriness in the accumulated clouds which shall light up the sea at night with another and more terrible splendour. All these other facts Hunt could get into his picture 'because painting is a great intellectual art; an art of compensation and compromise and contrast, an art capable of moderation and subject to mastery.' And all these other facts Gustave le Grey could *not* get into his photograph, because photography is not a fine art, but an art science, narrow in its range, emphatic in assertion, telling one truth for ten falsehoods, but telling always distinctly the one truth that it would be able to perceive."

The fallacy of this will be easily seen. Hammerton takes, in the first place, the production of a perfect master in art, and compares it as an artistic production with the work of one who would never have asserted that he was the equal of Holman Hunt. He puts a comparatively new producing process, full of difficulties and drawbacks, and one still passing through infantine stages of experiment and discovery, in contrast with a very old one, which has been the outgrowth of centuries of progressive practice. He forgets that productions of the very art which he glorifies so proudly, and which Holman Hunt practised, could be produced vastly inferior to Gustave le Grey's photograph. Look at the great difference there is between photographs of light, air and perspective produced now, and those produced in 1872, and then tell me if that alone is not sufficient to demonstrate the lofty possibilities of their producer's art-science, when it is cultivated as "an art of compensation and compromise and contrast, an art capable of moderation, and subject to mastery." This will come when photography is practised as a fine art, not as a mere amusement or as an uninteresting mechanical operation; when in the superior works of great artists, photographers find inspiration, not despair.

But let us go back to the defects complained of in Le Grey's picture as compared with Hunt's. I think you may see that they chiefly resolve themselves into a want of aerial perspective, or, in other words, a want of light and air. A well-known artist (Mr. A. Liebert), referring to this subject, says:—" One of the greatest difficulties of the landscape photographer is the production of skies ; instead of uniform whiteness producing a monotony which deprives the landscape of its aerial or natural perspective ; when all the delicate tones produced by distance and the reflection of the clouds disappear, and the image thus loses a great part of its artistic value."

In a cheap and not particularly comprehensive little work on aerial perspective, written by a professor of perspective, Wyke Bayliss, he says, "The great object of aerial perspective is to enable the painter to give his work that effect of light and shade and colour, which in nature is accomplished by the various objects of which the scene to be represented is composed." In securing any or all of these, aerial perspective may certainly be useful. More or less air between your camera and too prominent objects, will very often make wonderful alterations in the general pictorial effect. Something that is aggressive and impudently bold, distracting the eye from where you desire it to be attracted, may in this way be made quiet and inoffensive. The full rich variety of tones and forms which have so much to do with beauty may be in like way secured. Selecting one kind of aerial effect in preference to another, may give due dominance to the heroic part of your composition, and by mere contrast render objects that were in dangerous rivalry subordinate.

The amount of space which should be between the landscape painter and the base line of his proposed foreground is generally estimated at fourteen feet, to secure a transcript having forty-five degrees, and bring within the top and bottom of it any object not of greater height than sixteen feet, whatever the picture's size may be. But in photographing, this law will be affected by the lens used and the character and kind of foreground desired. Photographs may however be cut, and anything undesirable in immediate foregrounds may therefore be very easily removed by reducing the size or shape of the photograph.

Another consideration connected with aerial effect to be observed by the student in selecting time, place and scene, is the radiation of light at different hours and conditions from various surfaces. These sometimes generate very picturesque aerial effects of which you may often successfully avail yourself.

J. B. Pyne, writing on our present subject, says that an artist finishing his painting of a tree without having the original before him might easily spoil it, "not so much for want of knowledge and power over the local character of the object itself as from a want of those modifications of local character which result from the presence of a strong light and its different phenomena, radiation and reflection, and the distinction of those parts under partial, and those under perfect obscuration." A tree, for instance, seen in sunlight, although the foliage of both sides be equal in density will not seem so. On the lighted side the small twigs will be invisible and the next larger branches will be almost so; indeed, on this side all its forms will appear somewhat diffused and hazy. But on the darker side every branch, twig and leaf, will reveal itself with beautiful precision against the the sky. "But bring this shadowed part of the tree by change of position against a brilliant sunlit cloud, or let the sun be seen shining through it, and the dazzling radiations will make *it* as uncertain in its outlines, and blot out *its* details of stem, twig and branch." Such radiations are sometimes modified by aerial perspective. Some landscape etchings by Rubens suggest that he must have particularly admired such aerial effects.

Always then remember, as R. A. Leslie said in the early days of photography, that " Rocks, trees, mountains, plains, and water are the features of landscape, but its expressions are from above; and it is scarcely metaphorical to say nature smiles, or weeps, and is tranquil, sad, or disturbed with rage, as the atmosphere affects her." " And yet there are," as Leslie also says, many landscape painters (as there are many more photographers) who seem " as if they had never raised their eyes above the horizon ; and among the proofs of the indifference of those who interest themselves in art to the beauty that canopies the earth may be noticed that, although the composition and light and shade of clouds are as much within the reach of the photographic art as any of the other great things of nature, they are her only beauties it has hitherto entirely neglected. I have seen but two calotypes of skies, and these, taken by my friend Mr. Thurston Thompson, prove that it is from no want of power in the process that skies are not as common in our photographic exhibitions as any other subjects." If this was true when Leslie wrote it how much more true is it now when sky effects of the grandest character are successfully photographed?

The greatest landscape painters have been the most earnest students of light, atmospherical and sky effects. Turner's transcendent power of expressing aerial phenomena more than atoned for eccentricities that would have ruined a lesser man, and Constable spent entire summers in painting skies from nature. In a letter to a friend, dated October, 1821, he says :—" I have done a good deal of skying, for I am determined to conquer all difficulties, and that amongst the rest. That landscape painter who does not make his sky a very material part of his composition neglects to avail himself of one of its greatest aids. . . . It will be difficult to name a class in landscape in which the sky is not the key-note, the standard of scale, and the chief organ of sentiment." That which is true of Turner and Constable is true of all real art students. In the works of every truly great landscape artist we find the effects of sky, clouds, atmosphere, mist and vapour playing prominent parts.

Again quoting Ruskin (what higher art authority can one quote?), "We destroy both space and size either by the vacancy which affords us no measure of space, or by the distinctness which gives us a false one."

All these brief extracts from the works of practical eminent authorities will serve to show how important is the study of air and light to the landscape artist, whether painter or photographer. On hot sunny days the air is perceptibly in motion, and *all* objects seen through it have their outlines more or less completely blurred and indistinct where light is strong, although they are clear and well-defined where shadows fall. This phenomenon is full of beauty in nature. Turner often painted it, and engravings from his works tell us that the appearance it gives can be preserved in monochrome. I have known hundreds of photographers who, on one of these hot days, would only photograph a landscape in its shadowy passages, because in the sun-lighted passages objects wouldn't come out as they wanted them, clear, sharp and distinct. The confounded lens would insist upon fidelity to nature, and this bothered them. They knew all about clearness, sharpness and distinctness; they knew nothing about nature's most admirable, poetical and picturesque effects of light and atmosphere.

One of the great charms of sunlight in this slightly vaporous condition is a blotting out, or subordinating of those too prominent yet pretty details which in photographs so often attract the eye from things of far greater importance. The dominant value of our best art exhibitions rests in the fact that, as a rule, they do not only show us what we may attempt and what we should avoid, but above all what we may achieve. So with all the fine arts, example is better than precept, and thus "in the sister art, poetry" (says a modern painter), "the perusal of the immortal writings of the mighty dead has kindled in many a soul a flame which had else been unlit," so that a just appreciation of principles which have governed the works of great masters is extended by "the facilities which are now afforded all classes for seeing and studying them." The office of the most earnest instructor is simply that of advocating what they practised.

> "Nature's sweet care to all her children just,
> With richer treasures and an ampler state
> Endows at large whatever happy man
> Will deign to use them."
> —*Akenside.*

CHAPTER VII.

ON WATER AS AN ELEMENT OF PICTORIAL EFFECT.

THE great Italian artist, Leonardo da Vinci, when advocating the habit of studying nature at all times, said that a painter should never be without his tablets on which to jot down suggestive, useful facts. The advice he gave painters, photographers may take with the same certainty of benefitting by it. More particularly is this a valuable and desirable practice when water is to be represented, for its expressions and conditions change with such subtle degrees and varieties of effect, that its faithful representation is at all times secured with great difficulty, whether we use pigments and canvas, or camera and chemicals.

But the opportunities it affords are in like way numerous. We have the bright, more or less rapidly flowing surfaces, its varying degrees of transparency and depth, the different reflections of earth and air, and hundreds of accidental circumstances, such as a ferry boat, a stately swan, cattle drinking, geese swimming, beds of rushes, water-lilies and weeds, a boat, boys bathing, the encircling ripples of a fly-catching fish, happy effects due to a movement of the camera to the right or left, backwards or forwards, upwards or downwards, the branches of fallen half-submerged trees, a fisherman in a punt or on the bank, the darkening of a reflected hillside, or a passing cloud, or even a stone thrown in, etc., all may be made helpful. Good examples of the introduction of cattle, boats and figures will be found in the two illustrations from engravings after well known painters, on this and opposite pages.

The most common faults in photographs of water are:—A want of transparency, the utter loss of all but a mere blank outline in the too strongly-lighted surfaces. Patches of meaningless white here and there, near and far, being the result, giving a spotty, eye-confusing effect altogether destructive of truth and

pictorial composition. A want of tenderness, transparency, delicacy and flatness shown where the darker reflections prevail. Sometimes an entire river goes winding its way through the landscape without a ripple or a single reflection, as if it were a piece of white paper stuck down on the photograph. In this case it was probably taken in broad, bright, open sunlight, lamentably over-exposed and developed by some human machine as unobserving, unsympathetic and unimaginative as the camera itself.

A grey, quiet day seems the best time for lake and river scenery, and in many instances such an atmospheric condition will lend itself harmoniously to the general character. But in all cases the artist should let the characteristic effect of the actual scene decide its treatment; in other words, he should not shirk a difficulty if by so doing he sacrifices sentiment and feeling.

Quiet pastoral valley scenery amidst low-lying hills, fields and meadows having an idly meandering

river for its dominant feature can be helped by securing everything that is associated with ideas of repose and tranquility. The lights and shades should blend tranquilly; nothing should be staringly prominent or loud, nothing too energetically active. If you have a fisherman with companions let none be talking or let him be lonely and restful, placidly watching his float, not even throwing a fly. If you choose any other figure, let it be one with a book under a tree, and if you have two figures let them be palpably lazy, lingering lovers, *whispering* as if unwilling that even a passing zephyr should catch their ardent words. Allow no noisy, romping children to appear in such a scene, no passenger be in the act of shouting for a ferry boat, no sportsman discharging his gun. All these features may be desirable in other scenes, but here they would be out of keeping, would destroy a special and desirable sentiment. Anything that will indicate that the spot depicted is an unfrequented one will aid. Let the distant hills melt *tenderly* into air; let the flow of the water suggest its *gentlest* murmurings, such as hot, dry, *languor begetting* weather brings. Keep the line of the horizon low, and so on and so on. To enforce this view I may add that just such an effect as would harmonize with such a river scene, Ruskin describes in his remarks upon a drawing of Ulleswater, made probably in 1808, by Turner.

The great critic says:—"The lake is quite calm; the western hills in grey shadow, the eastern massed in soft light. Helvellyn rises like a mist between them, all being mirrored in calm water. Some cows are standing in the shallow water in front; a boat floats motionless about a hundred yards from the shore. . . . This was evidently Turner's record of a quiet evening." The painter afterwards made a more finished painting from this very study, but its feeling and expression were not disturbed. We have in it, as in the original sketch, as Ruskin says, "the same hills, the same shadow, the same boat and the same cows. They have stood in his mind as they stood on the same spot, for twenty years." Just that strong impression which in nature they left upon the painter's imagination, they still leave upon the minds and hearts of those who look at them in his picture.

In this we see how Turner preserved his observations

for future use, as Da Vinci said a painter should. The quiet cattle chewing their meditative cud, with their not less placid reflections, the tranquil, soft grey shadows sleeping on the hill-sides, the lazily rising mist and the boat at rest, all these are what the artist calls accidents or accessories, and in all of them we recognise a strengthening of the one leading idea, strongly emphasizing the main characteristic of the painting. Everything therein is powerfully suggestive of softness, gentleness, quietude and solitude. We know how in other scenes this true poet-painter adopted other ideas. In one we find all the accidents and accessories speak of active energetic action, of life and its business aspects; in another everything is grand and stately and dignified, and in yet another everything that speaks of solemn gloom aids the dominating idea. For such a dominating idea of some kind or another every picture should have, as otherwise it is like "the play of Hamlet with the character of the Prince of Denmark omitted by particular desire." But in adopting this advice be careful to do so without overstepping the modesty of nature, without forgetting that the great aim of all art, poetical, dramatic or pictorial, is to conceal art.

We have lately had some eccentric doings in the printing frames. But remember that a bad photograph will never be made a good picture by merely printing it upon a uniformly grained surface, or rough drawing paper, or paper with a ridiculous regular staring pattern on it, or paper made to look like canvas, or the substitution for it of some textile fabric. Yet a paper which is tinted instead of white, rough instead of smooth, or which carries a graduating stipple of light into every part of the photograph, is—properly used—by no means objectionable, and may often be very advantageously used, not, however, *always*.

G

As for sea, lake, pond, pool, river or stream, whether they chatter with musical baby voices in the brook, or run in silent rivulets lost in the grass to which they give a fresher green; ooze from great reservoir beds of mountain moss or trickle down into the plains to become famous rivers; the treatment of such subjects should vary in the artist's work as strikingly as they do in nature. In all their forms, as in all their phases and diversified expressions, they delight the poet and the artist's eye and speak to them each in his own language. The unobservant, unimaginative and unpoetical may be deaf to their utterances, see nothing of any of these picturesque features: and what they do not see that they will, of course, never try to represent.

Mr. Thompson, an old photographic friend of mine, who photographed water with considerable success, said in one of his papers, "The weakness of photography in its representation of water is one upon which painters have not failed to enlarge . . . the sparkle, the transparency and beauty of living water is seldom seen. A dull, opaque lifeless blank of white paper is but too common a substitute for the representation of water."*

Water rushing impetuously down a rocky course, leaping the boulders and foaming between them, or water dashed headlong down in one vast sheet over the edge of a precipitous cliff would be quite unlike the quiet lake or river subject, and would consequently demand different treatment, such as we find it has received in the works of great painters.

---

* Pictures with a foreground of water should always be taken as much against the light as possible, as the shadows have then a depth and intensity which go far to equalize the illumination, and the water is not destroyed by over-exposure before the rest of the subject has impressed its image on the sensitive plate.

WATER. 99

If we follow the course of a rushing stream, foaming and swirling, dashing and leaping, in and out and round about, over jagged sharply angular edges of rock, throwing up spray, forming here and there cascades, and

Australian Scenery.

From a drawing
by
Arthur James Wall.

Deep In a Fern-tree
Gully, and
High on a Hill Top
looking
towards the Sea,
Victoria.

here and there broadening out into pools which gleam out at you with a ghastly glare from dark interlacing boughs and thick foliage, or disappear in treacherous masses of swampy moss and mud, in each case we are impressed by special characteristics in a special way. Your photographs should convey the same impression. There we want no traces of human occupation, no sign of cottage or farm, cattle or cultivation, but everything suggestive of wild freedom and impetuous action. Masses of loose stones will suggest elemental warfare or the torrent's angry fury, and a few torn-away branches swept down with them may lend force. Obviously the effects to be watched and waited for under these conditions are those which lend force to ideas of gloom and terror, stony barrenness, and a silence unbroken by any voices but those of mournful wind and roaring water. Such and similar scenes the landscape painter finds in the wilder parts of Cumberland, Cornwall, Devonshire, Yorkshire, Westmoreland and Wales, Ireland and the Scottish Highlands. They are, like pastoral solitudes, lonely, quiet, and solitary. But yet how different! Sharp, abruptly broken angles have taken the place of flowing lines softly melting one into the other; strong abrupt contrasting lights are seen instead of softly mingling half-tones, and the deep, sudden shadows of cavernous hollows and overhanging precipices have taken the place of less pronounced *chiaro oscuro*. Who shall say, when these picturesque effects are secured in photographs that the art cannot make others think and feel as poets and painters make them think and feel, or that they are not works of art? That such photographs can be secured is now too well known a fact to be honestly disputed.

Pencil Sketch.
Composition of Trees and Water

River subjects are abundant and nearly always beautiful. Who that has wandered along the banks of the Wye cannot recall a panorama of changeful river scenery in which there was a constant diversity of incident, interest and picturesqueness? And along the banks of the Thames from London Bridge to the Nore, or to Richmond and Windsor, what a wealth of subject matter awaits the camera, changing with almost every yard of progress. How well, too, the beauty of Thames scenery has been recognised by great painters. What strange and curious stories are associated with it. What phases of human labour and life, how romantic are its best known traditions and history. Nor should Shakespeare's river, the "soft flowing Avon," be forgotten.

Pencil Sketch.
A Composition of Trees and Water.

And then again the sea. What a world of novelty and freshness has yet to be harvested in our pictorial records by cameras, on waves or shore, by artists with eyes quick to see what the trained perceptive powers teach them to look for, scenes of storm or calm, might and majesty. Recall what Stanfield and J. C. Hook have done in this direction, and aim high even if you hit low. There is one hint which I will add, because it comes from practical experience. When photographing sea waves, so place the camera that the angle at which the light reaches it from the waves

Pencil Sketch.
Composition of Wood and Water.

conveys it in a softened condition, and the reflections in the shadowy passages are not sacrificed or lost to sight. The reflections in this state have greater actinic power.

In the late P. G. Hammerton's "Painters' Camp in the Highlands" you will find some gloriously suggestive chapters on the pictorial treatment and characteristics of water, in which he dwells upon rocky streams, upon storms on the lochs when the black waves flecked with white yeast leap five feet high and look higher. Of dim monotonous grey landscapes, of the rain-squalls that cover the lakes from shore to shore "with a sharp line of ghastly grey that advances in all its breadth over the great black cauldron of waters as fast as charging cavalry;" of ravine torrents; of the wild fierce rush of mountain streams on the hill sides; and of days when "the lake lies stilled to sleep, reflecting every isle and every tree along the shore, its bright surface dimmed here and there by faint breezes, that remain each in its place with singular constancy, as if invisible angels hovered over the waters and breathed upon them." Of dark unfathomable calms under the great mountain with such an expression of peace and repose that looking at it sleeping so calmly in its deep bed you can hardly believe that "but yesterday this shining liquid plain was covered with ten thousand crested waves, and countless squalls struck it all over like swooping eagles. It seems as if this solemn calm had been its condition from the foundation of the world and would be thus for ever and for ever."

Describing how he stood upon the Bridge of Cladich he says (and this passage is full of hints for the photographer): "The water is very wild and very fierce and very strong, yet not lawless, for it follows certain forms with wonderful fidelity. The rocks under it dictate the form of its flowing, and the water steadily obeys. Yet there appear to be little periodical pulsations and variations from the law caused by subtle minor laws. Thus I perceive that a certain jet of spray is thrown up every quarter of a minute or so at a particular spot as regularly as the action of a steam engine, and at certain stateable intervals a wave on the shore rises three inches higher, then subsides to its own level. In spite of the rapidity of this flowing torrent there are parts of it nearly at rest except their own ceaseless circling in deep holes at the side. There are great lumps of thick yellow yeast in these places whirling round and round. The colouring of the water is full of fine browns and yellows, good, tawny, rich colouring with creamy white at one end of the scale and something like fire opal at the other." It would perhaps be easier to realise such a scene as Hammerton here describes, or parts of it, with the camera than with the painter's tools and opportunities, but in either case the task would be one of no little difficulty.

Again, still speaking of Highland landscape, he tells us of pictures to be got of the deep brown pools of a stream at rest, " very deep, very smooth and very quiet; pale golden at the shallow side where not an inch of water covers the smooth pebbles, then darkening as the water deepens through all the shades of gold and brown to something darker and more terrible than mere blackness. Out of this, and all around it, rise grey rocks."

He says of Highland scenery generally, "this country is a wonderfully great and noble school for landscape effect;" of Glen Urchay, its broad salmon streams and its great curving banks of rich green low-land contrasting, brown, barren hill sides, and of its waterfalls that they are "as good as those our landscape painters bring us from Norway." Of the way in which the water shapes out the rocks he says, "Every true painter has an intense perception of some fragment of natural truth that nobody else seems to care for, but it is really astonishing that the exquisite beauty of water *sculpture* should have been so little felt by the most celebrated men. Turner only cared for it occasionally, and never enough to paint it in full and perfect detail. Of all our living landscape painters there is only one who seems to enjoy the kind of sculpture which such a stream as the Urchay can accomplish in innumerable years. Mr. Petitt paints it faithfully."

In his " Painting from Nature " this same thoughtful and earnest art-student and lover of Nature recommends lowland France as a field and says, "on the banks of the river Yonne, it is possible to work from Nature as many days in one year (Scotch weather being so capriciously unfavourable) as you would get in seven years in the Highlands."* And the French subjects if not so grand are infinitely *prettier,* infinitely easier to deal with, and I should imagine could be worked up into more popular pictures.

*Sitting hour after hour and day after day at the easel in open air is one thing, however, and exposing a few plates in the camera is another. Here again the advantage is on the side of photography.

CHAPTER VIII.

OF SENTIMENT AND FEELING, CONTRASTS AND
VARIETY, SUBORDINATION, DOMINATION
AND HARMONY.

IN an American magazine called *The Forum* (what excellent things these American magazines are), Mr. Harrison speaks of the French school of painting in our day as a degenerate one. It gives us, he says, "mere coloured photographs without grace, pathos, awe, life or invention." They are "as ugly, as crude, as photographic, as unpleasant as canvas and dull paint can make them. . . Everything is flat, angular, prosaic." Again he says, "Some hold that art means utter dulness and strict elimination of every source of interest. A dirty old woman vacantly staring at a heap of stones; a pig wallowing in fetid mud; a dusty high road between two blank walls; a sandbank under a leaden sky—such are the chosen spectacles dear to rising genius." There is undoubtedly, as he says, an idea largely prevalent amongst modern artists, English as well as French, that "art needs no inspiration, no ideals, no guidance, no thought, no beauty, no self-control; that its sole task is to put on canvas whatever is to be seen." And this, he adds, "is the broad road that leadeth to destruction."

I don't think I could have found a better text than this on which to base my present chapter. Suppose, now a photographer, alive to the necessity of artistic culture, but ignorant of its principles, seeks to learn by imitation—that broad, well-trodden, smooth and easy road. He is smitten with the works of modern French painters of the class Mr. Harrison denounces, mainly because they aspire to nothing beyond the reach of his unthinking, unimaginative, faithfully reproductive lens. The highest qualities such painters aspire to are just those in which a well-exposed, good negative and a carefully printed positive can beat them hollow. The first dirty old woman the photographer meets will stare vacantly enough for his purpose, and heaps of stones can be found by every roadside. He photographs her as the French artists painted her, simply as she is, and thinks he can thus produce a work of art because he has seen just such a painting in a picture gallery. And so true to life! But would Wilkie have done this thing? Can't you imagine what that old woman would have become in this hands? With what tender-heartedness he would have conceived the story of her outcast loneliness, her footsore weariness, the often darned and mended rags no longer mendable, the nearly soleless shoes, and and in her poor, thin, withered, wrinkled face, a world of pathetic meaning. The dull eyes so mournfully introspective; the poor, thin, bony limbs, so little like flesh; the hollow cheeks, the toothless gums, and the stale crust taken from her bundle for a meal in the gathering twilight of fast approaching night. And this would be a picture, perhaps a poem—for pictures are poetical when artists are poets. But what would all this mean? Feeling and imagination, the seeking for a fit and appropriate model, the gathering together of all these story-telling incidents for the one purpose, that of making not merely a painting or a photograph but a picture.

Therefore, before beginning a subject think about it and don't hurry the process. Exhaust every idea that has a bearing upon it; seek inspiration in all works akin to it in spirit and design; let your imagination first depict it; let your feelings imbue it with life and warmth before you place it in front of your camera, or your camera in front of it. Put sentiment and feeling into it, that sentiment and feeling may come out of it into the hearts and minds of the thousands who will see it. He who takes up his camera as he would a chisel or a spade may be an excellent operator, and by some lucky accident may occasionally produce a prize-winning picture; probably because the model or scenery he photographed could not possibly make anything but a picture. Yet he is no artist. This, his less fortunate productions or the bulk of them will suffice to demonstrate.

A dear, dead friend of mine, a photographer and painter, whose works and memory are still treasured amongst us, O. G. Rejlander, would think about and talk and study for a subject months before he produced it photographically. His photographs, as photographs, are generally more or less defective, but sentiment and feeling abound in them, as they did in himself. His love for a pretty child or a beautiful woman inspired him with feelings akin to them—poetry and music were in them— the poetry that made him gentle and tender to them, and the music of his lines and tones, if but that of the eye, was as subtle in its influences, as varied, as sweet, and stole as readily into the heart as if it had found admission by the ear.

Even a graceful line gradually swelling upward into boldness and curving meltingly down into its lower and more tender gradations, or a like combination of graduated tints and tones, is fairly representative of musical notes cunningly combined in a delightful composition. And in like way a combination of abrupt angles may represent louder, sharply contrasting and more wildly stirring effects akin to other kinds of music. The feeling in production is the same. The sentiment of form is associated in effect with that of sound. The portrait of a graceful and beautiful woman, the unstudied simplicity of a pretty child, the dignity of some venerable old man, the strength and manliness of the warrior, the stateliness of royalty, and the solemn dominance of the ecclesiastic, each subject has its own appropriate sentiment and feeling. As the musician expresses them by his notes so the artist does on his canvas, in his marble, or with his camera. The music may be that of the eye or ear, its power is the same, and, practically the results are the same. Rejlander used to say that music inspired some of his best thoughts, and I remember how on one occasion as my wife played a sweet piece of music full of pathetic power, he followed the rise and fall of the notes by a line that rose and fell in the same low, gliding way, and in the end shouted with gleeful triumph to see how forcibly the sentiment and feeling of ear-music realised that of the eye-music. I believe he afterwards reproduced those lines in the pose of a charming young girl's figure and the arrangement of her "drapery" (as artists say), and that I made and published a drawing from it in one of the art magazines.

Landscapes, treated artistically, call for the same qualities. The rugged and rocky, the wild and woody, the bright and cheerful, the gloomy and solemn, the stern and the pensive, all express sentiments and produce feelings in harmonious relationship with musical expression. Lines, tones, aerial and light effects, etc., etc., may all be regarded as means to this end, because all have their associated ideas, sentiments and sympathies. Tones may also be used as harmonizing elements where they are grouped together without reference to suggestive meanings, as notes of music are sweet without words. The loud, stirring strains of a warlike march, and the soft languishing notes of a love song, the solemnity of the anthem and the plaintiveness of a mournful ballad, would be as palpably what they are if they were never sung or never marched to. So in a picture, tones are composed to represent certain things, but also to convey pleasing combinations of pictorial elements that in one way or another delight the eye only. Artists thus find in them wonderful additions to their powers.

Years ago I often used to hear photographers talk about exposing for this or that kind of negative because they liked their effects. But they were seldom artistic. They could not as a rule be made to understand that they should really expose for natural effects only; that in one picture masses of strong darks got by short exposure and long development would be fatal to the sentiment of strongly-diffused light and delicately tender sun shadows. No matter what the time of day, month or season chanced to be, their negatives were always bright and strong, brilliant and forcibly defined. The test was always the negative's perfectly artificial density in the high lights and the as perfectly transparent shadows. They never looked for the subtle gradations of tones nor remembered how valuable ideas associated with them were for expressing sentiment and feeling. They never imagined that what was true and good in one case could in another be bad and false; that when photographs taken under a wide range of varying natural conditions were all alike in the tones of their light and shade, they were necessarily all alike in their falsity to both art and nature, because wanting as nature never is in sentiment and feeling. The association of ideas is to them, perhaps for want of ideas, something of no practical value. I have heard in the lonely silence of the wild Australian bush the screaming cry of a night bird or some other animal, perhaps a dingo, that made the blood run cold. And yet it only meant perhaps hunger or thirst, or a signal cry. I knew this; but the sound, from its more terrible associations, was none the less terrible. These things show us how perfectly real the power of associated ideas is, and what nonsense it is to ignore their existence. "A genuine metaphor," says one of my dear old Shakespearean friends—Joseph Skipsey, the widely-admired Newcastle poet—"is always the outcome of something more than mere fancy, and may have the deepest significance." In this way a moan, which is the sign of sorrow, affects the hearer with sorrow; while a groan, or a series of groans, which arising from anguish strongly affects and oppresses the hearer, may do so to such an extent as to throw him into a state of anguish, whether the sound proceeds from a man who is choking in the gasp of death, or from an old oak straining under the oppressive grasp of the hurricane. Again, a sweet tone puts us into a sweet disposition, a state of things identical with that from which it proceeds, whether from the lips of a beautiful woman or from the mouth of a sweetly-tuned musical instrument. For "sounds as well as colours and forms have their manifold significations." And the very lines and tones, lights and shadows of an artistically-composed picture move us in like ways through like causes. Works of art have uses beyond the representing of forms and surfaces to the eye. It is their purpose to convey thoughts, to awaken ideas, and by increase of wisdom to make nature at once more understandable, more divinely wonderful, and more tenderly loveable in the minds and hearts of all mankind.

There is another point of view from which it is desirable we should consider the present subject, one of no small importance. It concerns what the artist calls subordination and domination of parts with reference to the general effect. In the act of observing any natural scene or object, whether it be landscape or figure subject, the mind is simply and absolutely occupied at any given instant of time by a definite single conception, the effect not of separately observed parts, but of parts seen in unity, combined as a whole. Directly the eye ceases to take in the entire view and to be focussed upon any particular part of it, large or small, instantly the effects of the parts have gone. For it is impossible to see objects collectively and separately at the same instant of time, although owing to the rapidity with which the observing power of the mind is successively influenced, this fact is not generally recognised.

From it partly we derive the principle of making all the elements of a picture subordinate to some general effect, which is in turn subservient to the artist's dominant idea, that which every part helps or should help to express. To unite these elements we seek what is called Harmony, a quality for which contrast and variety are essential. The word harmony is a word of Greek derivation, and implies consistency in combination, that which Ruskin calls a source of power and grandeur, uniting sentiment or feeling with propriety and simplicity. Priestly spoke of the same idea in poetry when he wrote critically, " No digression can be said to be unexceptional that doth not connect equally well at both ends with the piece to which it is introduced." Hogarth, too, says of painting, " Fitness of parts to the design for which every individual thing is formed, either by art or nature, is first to be considered." And Henry Howard, R.A., in one of his Academy lectures, said:—" To produce an agreeable effect every part must bear a varied and proportionate relation to all the rest." To blend variety and contrast so as to produce unity of effect, sentiment and feeling, is then the end which all the previous chapters of this series have so far advocated.

Sameness and monotony would soon result from the absence of variety and contrast. Contrasting sentiments, thoughts and images would be powerless, ungoverned by some dominant quality. A very suggestive illustration of contrasting elements in combination, which will help to make my meaning more clear, is found in the following lines, from Thompson's "Season":

> "The cottage hind
> Hangs o'er the enlivening blaze, and, fateful, there
> Recounts his simple frolics. Much he talks,
> And much he laughs, nor recks the storm that blows
> Without, and rattles on his humble roof."

Here depicted with the greatest simplicity we have cold and darkness contrasting the warmth and light; the fierce, angry storm without, and quiet peace and safe shelter within; the moaning, melancholy, shivering winter wind, and merry laughter; the suggested thought of outcasts cowering in the blast, and the jocund stories of the cheerful fireside group. Each contrast is perfectly harmonized by the dominant idea. The previous lines of this poem are also very suggestive.

In music, as in poetry and painting, the same principle is developed, contrasting notes forming parts of harmonious combinations.

"Painting," wrote Simonides, "is but mute poesy; and poetry, speaking painting," and form and colour in painting, he might well have added, are but music and poetry combined. "The brook at my feet," said N. P. Willis, "from its birth in the hills till it rested in the meadow's lap, tripped down like a mountain maid with a song unsullied by one harsh note." Such a brook in a picture should be as suggestive.

In architecture the same principles are found. What would the effect of a building be if deprived of its contrasting lines and forms or of their variety? Take a flat-faced, monotonous brick house of the worst modern type, a thing all angles of one kind, with square holes each exactly like the other set in straight rows for windows, a door always in one or the other of two places. Is this a thing of beauty? And if not, why not? Is it not because it lacks contrast and variety?

These are *principles* governing effects whatever be the method or manner of their production. Rules vary, and there is no exact way in which they should be adopted and carried out. It is not the way of doing this or that but the result which makes the landscape picture artistic or inartistic, and the success is obtained rather by the adoption of principles than by slavishly obeying laws and regulations laid down by other practitioners for their individual guidance. We may see in two pictures by two artists a certain aspect of nature painted under precisely the same conditions, and each a triumph. But assuredly they will differ in matters of detail, each will leave upon his work the stamp of his own individuality. In just the same way two men may copy in writing a piece of poetry, but their handwritings will not therefore be exactly alike. Photographs too often imitate both words and handwriting, expressing no individuality to distinguish one man's work from another's.

CHAPTER IX.

PICTORIAL COMPOSITION.

THE word composition, pictorially applied, embraces almost everything that belongs to artistic design. It is a word of wide application with many elements, and has its foundations on principles as soundly scientific as those which belong to the construction of a building, a piece of music, a play or a poem. It is, however, a word which is frequently wrongly understood. It does not imply, as some too hasty reasoners often conclude it does, the separating and recombining of fragments not naturally associated. This was one of the earliest mistakes made by photographers. And hence we had all kinds of incongruities, a confusion of conflicting facts and ideas, a frittering away of good effects, and a medley of selected things that harmonized neither with themselves nor with any one dominant artistic purpose.

Then again, there are others who imagine it to be a word of technical meaning and mechanical application, a very simple affair indeed. With them to put a large jug between two little ones, as some cottage dame would intuitively arrange them on her chimney shelf, is to compose. With others composition is a scattering of numerous accessories around some central object, merely because they are in themselves pretty, and, it may be, interesting, whereas they only distract the observer's attention and confuse his sight. They do not compose, they decompose a picture.

How often, looking at some combinations of trees, rivers and mountains, or some figures accidentally grouped, the painter or sculptor will exclaim, "how gloriously they compose!" This is because he understands what composition is. It is not, again, as some suppose, purely fanciful, the result of neither reasoning nor observation, for it comes only from both. Neither dexterous manipulations, nor skilful focussing, nor careful development will secure composition in the works of one ignorant of artistic principles, although each will aid composition. The shifting of a camera stand a few yards to the right or left, backward or forward; the raising of it or depressing it; the presence of a few apparently most unimportant accessories introduced by sheer accident—all these things may make or mar the composition according as you do or do not recognise their influences. It all rests with yourself. The eye sees no more than it brings with it the power to see. That little cat at court who recognised neither the signs of power, grandeur, nor dignity, but had a quick eye for

"The little mouse under the chair,"

was as blind to splendour as a photographer inartistically trained is to the finest specimen of composition in landscape or figures. He too sees only the little mouse he wants to catch. The painter might as logically expect to do without composition by inventing some medium of rare value for his pigments, or some particularly good colours, as the photographer may by chemical and optical studies unaided by artistic study. The best advice the best artist can give the beginner in art is to examine the works of the best masters critically and then go to nature and look for what they saw. Look and think. Think and look. "Practice," said Sir Joshua Reynolds, "is justly called *purblind*, for practice that is tolerable in its way is not *totally* blind, an imperceptible theory which grows out of, and accompanies, and directs it, is never wanting to a sedulous practice; but this goes a little way with the painter himself, *and is utterly inexplicable to others.* To become a great proficient, an artist ought to see clearly enough to enable him to point out to others the *principles*

Specimen of Pictorial Composition.   From an Engraving.

on which he works, otherwise he will be conventional, and what is worse, he will be uncertain." Composition is no mere adventitious thing adopted to bestow factitious graces and artificial charms, it is a part and parcel of imitative art, essential to successful and truthful representation. The phenomena of nature defies re-creation; we can at the best but feebly imitate, and to aid our efforts every power available is an absolute necessity. He who has such powers in the greatest abundance is the greatest artist.

The works of many eminent old masters in art are rather illustrations of what we should avoid in composition than what we should apply; they are so fantastical and eccentric. A green landscape was, for instance, an abomination in the eyes of certain landscape painters in the last century. With them it was always autumn, and a picture without a brown tree in it was regarded as a glaring example of very bad composition. Now some of the most delightfully brilliant and cheerful compositions on the walls of our picture exhibitions are composed in the richest variety of fresh, spring-like sunny greens. The leading principle in composition is *unity*—unity of intention or purpose, unity of sentiment or feeling. Every outline, whether real or indicated by the boundary of vision, every point of light or dark, all the intermediate tones, and every object the picture embraces, may concentrate the power and purpose of the artist into a focus, or weaken and destroy it. All these things are expressive, each says something to the mind of the spectator, and it is your business to make them blend as alto, bass, tenor and soprano blend in the harmonious composition of the musician, with, of course, due reference to the dominant key. If all such things are not associated with them in the view before your camera, alter its position so that in one way or another they do not appear on your focussing screen. In this way you realise a dominant idea, to which everything in the picture is subordinated. A different scale of tones, arrangement of lines, lights, shades, masses, points, etc., for a different scene, but for this nothing that does not belong to its pervading sentiment, nothing that will not compose or harmonize therewith and give pictorial effect.

PICTORIAL COMPOSITION.   119

Those rules of art which accepted authorities have laid down for practical guidance are of great value to the student. They are very suggestive, they simplify practice and economise time and labour. But followed blindly, with a kind of superstitious faith in their importance, they mislead and are mischievous. The artist-photographer should always remember that he is working under conditions and with methods unknown to those who

Specimen of Pictorial Composition.   From an Engraving.

founded such rules. His practice, although in aim it is one with the picture painter's, is yet so distinctly his own that it becomes a positive necessity to modify and adapt for his use, rules which were originally formulated for disciples of a sister art.

It is, therefore, doubly necessary for the camera artist to understand not only those rules which should govern his practice, but also the principles from which they spring. Otherwise he will be too apt to be slovenly and careless, to regard these things as matters of slight importance, merely as questions of taste, instead of scientific demonstration. It is his business to have a thorough conception of their actual and relative importance, their capacities, and their various applications. He should be able to explain how they act, and re-act one upon another, how they may be blended and how separated, and even when it is true wisdom to ignore them altogether. They are not intended to do away with the necessity of thinking, but to beget thought.

By way of illustrating what I mean, let us turn to one of the best known and most famous pictures in the world, Leonardo da Vinci's "Last Supper." In this any superficial observer with a knowledge of certain pictorial rules, which are amongst the oldest, simplest and best known we have, will see how they have been altogether set aside, and with advantage. If, instead of beauty, variety, contrast, breadth, and harmonious relationship of parts, Leonardo had sought only ugliness, sameness, monotony, spottiness and conflicting elements intended to confuse and distract the vision of all beholders, he could hardly have adopted a more suitable process of combination. Yet the result is glorious. The picture has been so often engraved that you are sure to be familiar with it. If you recall it to your mind, you will know we have in it, first, in the most prominent position, merely a long straight table, covered with a white cloth, standing on four conspicuous tressels, all exactly alike. There is a knot to each end of the cloth, each the size and shape of the other, and at either end its decorative border appears in seven thin straight upright lines, no more, no less. It (the table) runs straight from one end of the painting to the other, and the space left on either side is the same. The ceiling has square-edged plain beams and joints in abundance, formally intersecting each other at right angles and regular distances. Four angular pieces of drapery each of the same size and shape and equi-distant, hang straight and without a fold to break the repetition of their straight-pattern lines made up from the endless repetition of one simple ornament. At the back of the room are three angular openings, one large and two smaller ones, all precisely alike. Little loaves are arranged in a line along the top of the table, with a straight row of small drinking cups beyond them, all of one size and shape. Could you imagine anything more pedantically formal, more primitively simple? Can you conceive a composition more wanting in attractiveness or interest? It is almost like a *basso relievo*. The veriest tyro in art could point out its seeming defects, and show how the simplest and most elementary rules of composition had been violated in it by this great and glorious painter. But suppose this monotony and this want of interest was part of Leonardo's conception, and this apparent primitive simplicity of outlines, forms and *chiaro oscuro* were all intentional; that the artist determined to concentrate in one focus a marvellously dramatic story, realising in its fullest intensity the thoughts, feelings, incidents and characters belonging to it, and that therefore he thus subordinated every other part of the picture; that he ignored these simple elementary rules and carried out their principle upward to a grand development. Look at the picture again and study it from this point of view. See the Christ, isolated by the awe and reverence of His worshipping disciples, grandly simple in pose, God-like in the calm consciousness of His approaching agony and shame. He sits with His full face fronting you, exactly in the centre of the picture —where a well known rule says emphatically the principal figure should never be—and the disciples, divided into halves, sit six on either side—breaking another rule which has for centuries told us that in every group of figures some should have their backs to the spectator. Yet no more perfect or magnificent example of pictorial composition was ever conceived. It is a triumph of Principle. All the rules ever invented could not have helped Leonardo to anything half as perfect. Breadth of effect in treatment, and the concealment of subtlety

Specimen of Pictorial Composition. From an Engraving.

in design; variety of idea; force of expression; contrasts of pose, action and expression are all here. You never see those parts of the picture which were intended to be subordinated by their want of interest and unattractiveness. You see only that long straight row of human figures and faces.

But did Leonardo regard rules scornfully? By no means. Understanding principles he made from them new rules to suit emergencies. "Elementary principles,"

as Henry Howard, R.A., wrote, "which have been
correctly deduced cannot be changed ; but, happily, the
aspects under which nature presents itself to the eye and
sympathies of the painter, are infinitely various, and
leave different impressions on different minds. . . .
The precepts and practice of those great masters, from
whose standard productions our stock of theory is
derived," help us to understand the principles they
approved. If you want to know how Leonardo esteemed

Specimen of Pictorial Composition. From an Engraving.

rules, there is the book he wrote to tell you, illustrated
by himself, and published in his lifetime. " The young
student should," as his opening chapters assert, " study
Nature, in order to confirm and fix in his mind the
reason of those precepts, which he has learnt." He must
also bestow some time in viewing the works of various
old masters, to form his eye and judgment, in order that
he may be able to put in practice all he has been taught."
The organ of sight is one of the quickest we have, and

takes in at a single glance an infinite variety of forms; notwithstanding which, as I already have affirmed, we cannot perfectly comprehend more than one at a time. For example, the reader at one glance over this page immediately perceives it full of different characters; but he cannot at the same moment distinguish each letter, much less can he comprehend their meaning. He must consider it word by word and line by line, if he is desirous of knowing its meaning. In like manner, " if we wish to ascend to the top of an edifice we must be content to rise step by step, otherwise we shall never be able to attain it."

" I believe," wrote C. R. Leslie, R.A., " the advice every master would give to a young pupil, respecting his conduct and management of light and shadow, would be what Leonardo da Vinci has actually given, that you must oppose a dark ground to the light side. If Leonardo had lived to see the superior splendour and effect which has since been produced by exactly the contrary conduct, by joining light to light, and shadow to shadow, though without doubt he would have admired it, yet, as it ought not, so, probably, it would not, be the first rule with which he would have begun his instructions." Here again we find the *principle* in antagonism to the *rule*. " Now," says Leslie, in commenting upon this, "a very little observation of nature will show us that in her combinations, lights with lights and shades with shades are often united, and as often opposed."

Sir Joshua Reynolds was a great stickler for the observance of rules, and sometimes even went so far as to set up rules in opposition to pinciples. But in so doing his success is seldom, if ever, of an encouraging nature.

Leslie pointed out, in his " Handbook for Young Painters," another illustration of a rule ignored and a principle adopted. It was a painting by Watteau in the possession of Mr. Munro, " in which," as he says, "all the ordinary rules of contrast are departed from with a result as charming and as natural as it is novel. Two pretty little girls, bearing a twin resemblance, seem, from the difference of their sizes, not to have been twins, and it was no doubt the object of the painter to show as distinctly as possible their remarkable likeness to each other. He therefore placed them side by side, dressed nearly alike, in attitudes as little varied as possible, their faces seen directly in front, and with the same light and shadow. Indeed, all the usual contrasts of composition, expression, colour and *chiaro oscuro* are disregarded, yet the picture has not in any degree that formality that so often affects to pass itself for simplicity. Here the simplicity is real, and though Watteau seems not to have thought of the art or its rules, yet so consummate an artist was he that this production is not less legitimate than others of his works, while it is one of the most original pictures in the world." And he adds, " Watteau may possibly have been painting these little girls when members of the French Academy were excitedly proving Paul Veronese wrong in throwing a broad shadow over his ' Andromeda,'" because the hero of a piece ought, as a rule, to be always in full light.

Sir Joshua Reynolds, referring in the fourth of his Academy orations to this famous discussion, points out that the rule they regarded him as violating was not a law involving a principle, and said Paul had good reason for its non-observance.

I have selected to illustrate this chapter four engravings after paintings by famous artists, each an admirable example of composition. Their lines, the grouping, the lights and darks, and the general breadth are unmistakeably masterful. Dissect them and you will find that everything has its relative yet distinct value in their particular compositions. The lines which run into the space represented, or up, or at various angles, all aid the composition. So do the darks in their relative degrees of depth, size and position. We have in them *contrasts* of various kinds, and combinations of *blending* elements, all in like way subordinated to the main purpose. The degrees of interest are also parts of a whole, not *conflicting* or *detracting* one from the other. I might, of course, point out the details special to each, but in thus doing I should only be repeating the same things, and so I have thought it best to let them do their work in their own ways. They are all from paintings by artists of the greatest eminence, each a known master in the art of pictorial composition.

CHAPTER X.

THE COMPOSITION OF OUTLINES, AND THE POINTS OF VIEW.

AND now let us devote a few additional paragraphs to the subject of lines as elements of composition. We have already and more than once incidentally touched upon them from this view-point.

The artist-painter's outlines are veritable lines, but in his finished paintings they cease to appear as actual lines and become the boundaries of vision. There are, as one need hardly say, no outlines in nature, and there are none in a photograph. But the fact that the sight travels to and fro, up and down, out of and into a picture, along these boundaries of vision, makes them lines in effect, although they are not so in reality. They may be formed in many ways; by a band of light, such as a line of hills, the curves of a river, a wall, hedgerows, posts and rails, a flock of sheep, or a piece of pale drapery, or an outstretched limb, or trunks and boughs of trees, or tables, chairs, doors, windows, or many other things far too many for enumeration. In this way lines abound in pictures of every kind—curved flowing lines, abrupt angular lines, parallel lines, prominent staring loud lines, and quiet lines that modestly retire and are not seen until they are looked for. Artistically used they are all valuable aids to pictorial composition, or they are dangerous enemies to it, according as you govern or are governed by them. You have great power over all such things, if you only know how to use it. But they have great power too. By repetition, by prominence, by dominant tones, and in various other ways they may spoil your best effects utterly. Altering their perspective by concealment of parts, or throwing this or that out of strong light into deep shadow, may entirely change their aspect. By sheer dominance of repetition or by their inextricable confusion and equality of prominence they will often weary and perplex the eye. They can keep it from recognising the main idea or elements of superior importance, acting just as harsh, out-of-tune jangling will when it drowns the most carefully arranged notes of a subtle musical composition, or as a note out of tune will spoil the most finished harmony. In like way the lines of a building may, through want of composition, make that ugly which pictorial composition would have made beautiful. The principle is the same throughout art in all its varied elements and applications. The uses of lines are as fairly within the province of the art-photographer's studies as within those of the sculptor, painter or decorator. In like way they are valuable. They help you to give your ideas force, they can be made to call up feelings and sentiments in harmony with the general idea and purpose of your production. The mighty energy and sublime grandeur of Michael Angelo's figures and groups are splendid illustrations of the value lines have in works of art. "The Sistine Chapel," says H. Howard, R.A., "is an inexhaustible mine of study for the artist in this respect. His "Temptation of Adam and Eve" is (combined with "The Expulsion from Eden") in a vigorous and masterly style of composition, which had never been seen before his time. In this the concatenation of lines formed by the arms of the different figures is beautiful." The same able artist and lecturer on art describes Raffaelle's compositions as "often so artless in appearance that they look as if he had found them in nature, and sketched them on the spot. . . . His 'Deluge' is finely conceived and treated, the main line of figures crosses the canvas in a kind of chain." Speaking of that well-known work by Rubens, in Antwerp Cathedral, "The Taking Down from the Cross" (always admired as a piece of scientific composition), he says:—" The lines flow diagonally through the picture from top to bottom, that of the principal figure being the longest, which is still farther extended by the linen in which it is wrapped, carried out by the half figure at top, and combined with the kneeling Magdalene below. This main serpentine line, which illustrates Michael Angelo's axiom, is supported on one side by the large masses of St. John and the figure descending the ladder; on the other side, smaller portions of figures, finely varied, opposite the central stream of form, presenting altogether a beautiful example of concatenation, full of intricacy but simple, and One." You could not take away a line from this composition without weakening it. The eye goes perforce to the central figure of Christ, as the artist intended it should, every line from every quarter has here its focus, the eye cannot escape it. Lines that would have taken your attention from the central figure are broken with light and shade, or lost in gloom, while all the more important lines have full prominence given to them, but each in its degree. Nearly every great work of art, whether figure or landscape, will supply forcible illustrations of the importance of lines as elements of pictorial composition. I have seen a landscape converted from a dull, flat, uninteresting map into a deeply interesting picture by the introduction of a few figures, with one outstretched arm and pointing finger leading the eye to that part which was strongly suggestive of thoughts that appealed most forcibly to the feelings. It was the only way in which that part of the painter's subject could be made prominent, and it served its purpose fully. One light line, the arm running to a less prominent point, with a mass of dark to emphasise it, sufficed to make the striking difference that exists between a map and a picture.

One of the best and most practical of all our art student teachers, one I have already quoted several times, the late P. G. Hammerton, has told us that Turner's early career was commenced in an architect's office, where the full value of lines must have been strongly impressed upon him. For in no landscape painter's work will you find more instructive examples of powerful linear composition.

The same author says :—" There is an almost universal illusion that landscape painting is comparatively easy, an illusion which is based upon the truth that accurate drawing is not essential to a landscape painter. There are, however, other qualities than mere accuracy in good landscape painting, and other difficulties in the representation of nature than a simple definition of its forms. The greatest difficulty in this part of art may be expressed in a single word—complexity. The complexity of natural landscape is such that it cannot be understood, and therefore cannot be interpreted, without powers both of analysis and of synthesis, which a young student is not likely to have acquired. . . . In a climate so changeable as that of England, not only do effects change from hour to hour, and in distant scenery from minute to minute, but there is never any probability that if you go to a place on three successive days, exactly at the same moment, you will find your first effect again. Everyone knows how entirely different a place looks at different times. . . . To the mature and accomplished artist this changeableness of nature is an additional source of interest."

I have quoted this passage to show you that the camera man must depend upon intelligent and artistic observation for his composition, although he has really excellent opportunities of exercising his practical art knowledge by actual introduction of elements not supplied by nature or by any mere chance. But knowing and seeing are so intimately associated that he only sees what he ought to see, who knows how to recognise it when it is visible.

Another famous landscape painter, J. B. Pyne, in his splendidly practical " Letters on Landscape," advising a pupil who was then studying landscape-painting, says :—" In addressing yourself to nature it will necessarily more often be upon bended knee than *en garde*. She is not to be conquered but by the steadiest devotion, which becomes the rapid and spontaneous growth of the pursuit ; so that there is an equal danger of becoming her faithful though menial slave, as there is the chance, the glorious chance, of standing erect as her liberal translator. . . . You absolutely must confine yourself at setting out to the study of outline. You must take the term ' outline ' in its most extended and liberal sense, not as merely indicative of that manner of drawing which consists only of surrounding the forms of nature with a line, but as I have already shown, as indicating everything that takes possession of the spectator's eye, and carries it here and there at its own sweet will." Dwelling from another view-point upon the expressiveness of outline, the same writer says :—" The rounding off of a piece of country, a mountain, for instance— with all its variously-directed faces, its dimples or larger hollows, its risings and depressings, its bare brows and wood-matted sides, its ravines, scars and crags, with its many buttresses and firm seats in the lap of its own valley, up the sunny miles of which its sides may be traced—is not a thing to be represented as a screen with a hard edge, and is much more dependent upon judiciously-composed detail than upon either light or shade or colour. To instance one feature out of many, by way of illustration, take a deep hollow or depression in the side of a mountain wood. I choose this incident as its features are composed of objects of one character, size and form generally. There will, of course, be on the nearest side of the hollow a point, or rather a limit, which will form a defined outline against its opposite side. On approaching this outline the tree-tops will gradually become more frequent until they double on each other, and ultimately become involved in one outline with the lower and farther forms, so filling up the intervals between the next nearest that all indentation and undulation will be lost, presenting nothing more than a nearly even line, though not a sharp or well-defined one; while the nearest trees on the opposite side will come out in the full integrity of their forms and dimensions, sudden and distinct." Here we have just such an illustration of our subject as the photographer requires, and a better object lesson, so far as landscape goes in connection with linear composition, it would be difficult to hit upon. It is moreover a very suggestive passage for the old-fashioned photographic optician whose sole idea it so commonly is that equality of definition is the main thing, although it so often results in those sharp, equally-defined outlines of retiring surfaces which do not round off the hill tops but bring them out flat and upright like so many screens, nearest and farthest objects on their sides being inextricably confused, and which causes the remotest surface of a widely-extended plain to differ so little from the portion nearest the lens as to destroy all the natural effects of space and atmosphere.

The point of view is, of course, intimately connected with the angle of view. A landscape photograph should not embrace a larger field than the human eye takes in at a glance. In selecting the point of view, we therefore decide not only the angle at which outlines and surfaces will retreat from the eye to the point of sight, the point exactly opposite the point of view at the height of the spectator's eye, but we meet a variety of other considerations of no less value. The mind's perceptions are complicated with thoughts and feelings which they at once affect or create, and the pictorial artist's business is to bring them into order and concentrate all his forces with the art of a general arranging his army for battle. The point of attack is the point of superior importance in the warrior's case, and the artist in selecting a point of sight should take care it is not the point of least pictorial importance. When the eye of the spectator rests intuitively upon the artist's point of sight directly he sees a picture, then the other parts of it must fall each into its position of relative subordinance.

It would be excellent practice for students if some talented practical photographer, who is familiar with the pictorial mystery of his wonderful art as well as its scientific principles, would take out with him into the country a little band of beginners in artistic landscape photography; and setting up the camera for them, now here, now there, now at one height or angle, and now at another, now with one kind of lens, and then with a different one, would show them what a very striking important influence is exercised in a pictorial and photographic sense by the point of view. Linear perspective, aerial perspective, breadth, composition, *chiaro oscuro*, foreground, middle and extreme distance, contrast, subordination, harmony, everything that distinguishes a picture from a diagram depends upon it more or less. The dominant beauty of your view on one occasion is, say, the sky above it. There nature's smile is sweetest, there her loveliness is perfected, and there her voice speaks most musically, poetically or feelingly. In one way or another it is, you think, possible to photograph this sky. But certain cloud forms must be entire to have all it gives you, and if the camera is always to remain a certain height the horizon rising with it, as it naturally does, must so elevate the point of view that you will not get them. In another landscape it may be that the angle of view gives a point of sight so awkwardly situated that you have a petty, eye-confusing, spotty effect, instead of harmoniously blending tones and half-tones, lighted passages and shadowed, which another view-point secures by being placed at a different angle or elevation. Sometimes almost an inch higher and lower, to this side or that, will make wonderful differences. Chemically also the one view may be better than another for securing pictorial effect. It is almost impossible to develop certain negatives so as to secure the actual aerial effects and give each part its relative tones and values, because they are scattered and isolated, or in other and fewer words, when there are no broad picturesque features in the view selected. In like way, if the details of a subject are so uniformly and strongly illuminated as to come out with equal distinctness in your negative, you may sometimes escape that disagreeable inartistic effect by merely lowering the point of view, and so introducing foreshortening and other effects, tending to group some of them into masses and bring out others of most importance dominantly. Again, in photographing, say, a mountain lake, how often we fail because an overpowering brilliant surface of water radiating light at many angles, becomes a glaring patch of white paper (utterly unlike its glassy surface) in the print, through over-exposure and the effort to secure both deeply shadowed and strongly lighted passages. Limpid ripples and the delicate reflections of clouds and sky, mountain woods and precipitous rocks, weeds upon its margin and plants upon its water play their parts in close relationship with the point of view. The beautiful effect of a far-extending, delicate, wonderfully transparent wealth of shadow is often lost with the varied reflections, because we tried not to over-expose the lighted or under-exposed the shadowed passages, when a change in the position of the camera might have readily avoided both these difficulties. By elevating the point of view a desirable foreground may be brought into prominence to conceal the too brilliantly lighted surface, while contrasting and giving delicacy to the shadows and reflections and securing the beautifully graduated effects of space and air which we see in nature. A few yards in advance, a few paces in retreat will sometimes suffice to give the art-photographer a fair chance of getting all he requires to convert a poor, weak gathering together of disagreeing parts into a picturesque harmonious whole.

Of course, the view-point will not do everything; but it will be valuable in assisting you to acquire the most desirable results.

The negative may often be helped and improved for printing by artistic retouching with some transparent yellow or Indian ink with a little crimson lake in it, and these resources may also be wisely remembered, when considering the point of view. Every possible resource should be carefully considered with a view to their variously combined or separated actions, chemically and pictorially, when selecting from nature's vast abundance.

Too much study cannot be given to the considerations we have placed before you, but they are rather for practical experiments with the camera than theoretical instruction. Complicated when expressed in words and hard to explain, they are, nevertheless, comparatively simple in actual visual experiment. In every art, practice and experience are indispensable, and this is more particularly true of photography, an art so young and so rapidly progressive.

Colour again should step in to receive consideration when the view-point is being selected, because the tone representing one colour may constitute a discordant element chemically, while altering the time or view-point may exclude the difficulty, for colour as well as form differs under differing conditions of the light and air in connection with the view-point. If we can't fight we must run away. Adopt whichever plan meets your necessity most effectually, but always let the process be a result of careful thought. The status of photography cannot be elevated without intellectual effort; even in such an apparently simple process as selecting a point of view, there is a great field of study open in which you may worthily and profitably labour.

137

CHAPTER XI.

PERSPECTIVE, PHOTOGRAPHICAL AND PICTORIAL.

IN close connection with composition and the picture's view-point, as already stated, is the consideration of linear and aerial perspective. Messrs. Sutton & Dawson's well-known "Dictionary of Photography" says: "The rules of perspective merely relate to the cutting of pyramids by a plane, and are purely geometrical, not referring in any way to the structure of the eye, or the image formed upon the retina, or the rules of optics." "Perspective is," they also say, "nothing more than a very simple problem in solid geometry, and it is marvellous to find that so little is known of it by artists."

How little geometry has to do with pictorial perspective is readily seen in what architects call Geometrical Elevation, which, according to "Nuttall's Dictionary of Scientific Terms," is "a design for any part of a building drawn according to the rules of geometry as opposed to *perspective* or *natural* elevation." (The italics are the author's.) The term being derived from the Greek is also suggestive, for in that language it meant simply the art of measuring. It embraces the measurement of dimensions, lines, planes or surfaces, the contents of solid bodies and the functions of circles, in association with trigonometry, tetragonometry, polygonometry, cyclometry, etc., or, to speak more understandably and unscientifically, *angles* and *triangles*, *squares*, *many-sided forms*, *spheres*, *discs*, etc. Geometry existed in its elementary form in the days of the Chaldeans and Babylonians, but pictorial perspective is of comparatively modern origin.* The ordinary artist does not pretend to deal with the scientist's invisible, non-understandable lines, or " points " that have neither length, breadth nor thickness. And however far his imagination may or may not go in this matter, his business is simply the truthful and effective representation of visible objects. His points and lines *have* length, breadth and thickness, and are not practical impossibilities invented to define by signs what words alone cannot convey, dealing with things which are incapable of visible demonstration. They are not in his way, although they are so useful geometrically. The representation of forms on a plane surface, as they are conveyed through the eye and by the perceiving organs, is to him, as it is to the artist photographer, the chief purpose of perspective.

An old friend of mine, now, alas, departed, like so many dear old friends, in a volume which does not bear his name, for he was a bookmaker's hack, a publisher's " dark horse," defined perspective more clearly as " the art which enables us by fixed rules to represent truly on a plane surface that which appears to the sight in every variety of form and distance, and which is done by imaginary lines traversing such plane, and arranging the shape and position of every object with regard to the point of sight determined upon." This at once explains the extent to which geometry and perspective are allied in pictorial representation. In a like way geometry is allied to arithmetic, as in what is called geometrical progression (1, 2, 4, 8, 16, 32), for instance.

The owner of a good rectilinear lens with its diaphragms and a sufficient knowledge of the rules of

*Pictorial perspective was unknown until about the middle of the fifteenth century.

perspective to enable him to compare what he sees with the naked eye with what the lens sees, ought to be able to secure fairly accurate pictures, perspectively true and natural. He would in that case, probably, also come to the conclusion that focussing is a more important part of a photographer's work than he had previously thought it was, and that the only way in which a large photograph should be obtained, should be by enlarging from a small negative, and making a free after use of his scissors. It is true that by reducing the angle of vision the variety and extent of country represented in the photograph would be diminished, but the effect generally would be far less closely allied to optics and geometry, and far more closely allied to perspective and pictorial art.

"All improvements in composition," said C. R. Leslie, R.A., in one of his lectures, "from the infancy of painting to its full maturity are the result of the gradual discovery of the principles by which nature makes an assemblage of objects agreeable to the eye, those of perspective being amongst the most important." In further support of Leslie's view, Mr. Nuttall's view, Charles Martell's and my own, I may quote the words of Mr. Chapman Jones, a well-known scientific authority, who deals with the subject from a more purely optical point of view. He says, "The perspective of a picture as produced by any ordinary non-distorting photographic objective is correct when proper care is taken to keep the sensitive plate perpendicular, and will appear to be correct when viewed from a point having the same relation to the picture that the lens had during the exposure; but the picture will not appear exactly true to nature when looked at from any other point. The same limitation extends to pictures of every sort that represent solid objects." In taking a photograph he says, "the lens should be opposite the centre of the plate, so far as the possibility of moving it in a horizontal direction is concerned, unless there is a point of interest so strongly marked that it causes the attention to be concentrated upon it, when the lens may, with advantage perhaps, be brought opposite, or nearly opposite the centre of interest." Here science is not set up in depreciative opposition to art, but the two are allowed to be naturally allied, the one as the strong helper of the other, and both as blending harmoniously for the production of genuine pictorial effect. In point of fact, as I shall presently endeavour to show more clearly, what we have to seek artistically, is a compromise between what the lens sees and what the eye sees, for the two are not, as so many suppose, one, even in principle.

With eyes duly trained to see accurately, or more strictly speaking, to *perceive* accurately, a good knowledge of perspective will be quickly attained, and with it a desire to produce photographs more true, not so much to the actual facts of nature as to nature made visible by the eye to the mind, in other words, to the sense of sight.

"Stripped of its geometrical and mathematical intricacies," says Burnet,* "perspective will be found a very simple matter, and easy of comprehension, being nothing more than representing the various objects subject to the laws which regulate their appearance in nature." The photographer may commence its study by the aid of his lenses and camera, the artist with his pencil or brush, and both will find mastery of its principles and their applications, a source of pictorial power. To the landscape painter it is what anatomy is to the figure painter, discipline, training, knowledge and power. Even to the portrait photographer it is not less important.

* See his " Art Essays," published at the office of *The Practical Photographer*.

Place your tripod stand before a landscape view with buildings or retiring planes, and then watch the different aspects they assume as you alter the aperture and shift the focus from one plane to another. Then compare what you have seen under the cloth to what, standing where the camera stood, you see with the naked eye. You will at once note, if you have studied perspective, certain differences, more or less strikingly apparent, and understand how the drawing of a competent artist may be perfectly accurate, although it may at the same time be quite unlike a photograph taken at the same hour and under the same conditions of atmospheric light with a lens not stopped down and from precisely the same spot. You will know, moreover, why they are not alike; why in one picture the different planes of distance and outlines of forms are relatively incorrect; and why, in the other, they take their places naturally, expressing space and forms truthfully. It is largely the space between the objects and the lens, and the lens and the focussing screen, which gives accurate perspective, that is to say, pictorial perspective, as opposed to geometrical, scientific or purely optical perspective. The photographic *artist* of to-day focusses not to get either the most perfect chemical or geometrical focus, but to secure the natural, pictorial perspective. His predecessors had very little or no choice in the matter. Their cameras had one set distance at which the optical focus on the screen was as they said "sharpest," which sharpness was spread over every part of one plane, instead of extending in due and natural proportions to various retiring planes. In that way photographs were either geometrical diagrams flattened out of all truthful resemblance to nature, in order that they might illustrate the optician's knowledge of optical and geometrical science, or they were otherwise imperfect through distortion resulting from refraction. Straight lines were converted into curves, and the upper and lower surfaces of buildings made to appear disproportionately small or large, and consequently nearer to the eye than their centres were, etc. So in portraiture, the feet and hands were made disproportionately large, and even the ears and sides of a face thrown out of correct proportion for want of true perspective effect, and that too with lenses which opticians called perfect instruments giving geometrically-perfect perspective.

Another point which will illustrate my subject is found in the fact that images thrown upon the wall of a darkened room by light entering through a small circular aperture will give a view in which the perspective will not be geometrically or optically focussed on any one plane only, and with microscopical sharpness, but will be perspectively and pictorially accurate, giving space and atmospherical effects with truthful forms and proper relative proportions. This is significant.

I have already referred to the differences there are between what the one great glass eye of a camera reveals, and what our two small eye-lenses make visible; and that these can be demonstrated by the rules of pictorial perspective successively applied to drawings and photographs. But such differences are not more numerous, nor greater in kind, than those which may be readily enough discovered in the works of the most talented and experienced painters, representing the same view. For instance, recall what I have quoted—Mr. Hammerton's remarks on Turner's "Ben Cruachan," and upon another painting of the same view by Tripp.

Each of these was artistic and picturesque, but each was utterly unlike the other. The Turner was grand and glorious with effects of atmosphere and light, with mountainous forms of gigantic size and precipitous steepness. The Tripp was wild, rugged and romantic too, but without any such astounding exaggeration and flights of the imagination. In contrast Mr. Hammerton gave a purely topographical sketch made to show what the real view looked like and how unlike it was to both Turner's sketch and Mr. Tripp's, in making which as Mr. Hammerton says, " Turner was just as much an author of fiction as a poet in words, or a novelist." Of Tripp's picture he says, " He has been careful to preserve what seemed to him all the more important truths of local character. As I wander in Mr. Tripp's distance up Glen Strae, I remember many a real wandering in that region, and feel grateful to the artist for enabling me to live past days over again."

Fifty lenses of the same kind, used in one way, and placed one after another in this spot before the same view would all give strikingly similar pictures if photographed under ordinary good conditions. Equally well developed and printed from, each of fifty negatives thus taken would give fifty prints so much alike that you could barely tell one from another. There would have been even less likeness as a perspective illustration between Mr. Hammerton's topographical view, than there was between it and Tripp's more artistic picture, or between it and Turner's more wildly romantic and imaginative effects. The one would rouse wonder and delight, would excite by its passionate outburst of grandeur and marvellous realism—the other would carry your memory back to a spot you admired and loved, touching your feelings with sweet and tender recollections, arousing quieter and less powerful thoughts, whereas the tamely accurate topographical or the flattened and distorted photographical view would leave your imagination dormant, your feelings untouched. You would say calmly and coldly—" Yes, very true, I've been there, suppose it's like the spot, but somewhow it is not particularly interesting." Pictorial truth—pictorial qualities are not dependent upon absolute accuracy of any kind, local or other, although it is entirely the result of the greater and grander, or the more powerfully expressive truths of nature. And therefore I have been anxious while writing these chapters on Landscape Photography to impress upon students that they should use even linear perspective, a thing of mere mechanical measurement and accurate ruling from point to point, as subordinate to their search for effects of *chiaro oscuro*, composition, breadth, and the truths of sun and air.

The ordinary factologist or materialist receives on evidence with such blind faith as he gives to that of the senses. What he can see, touch, hear, taste, smell, are the foundations of his false, dogmatically narrow creed. If he happens to be a photographer of the mechanical type, and you talk to him about perspective, he turns a deaf ear to you. He regards human eyes and the optician's cameras as if they were perfectly similar instruments. Exactly as the healthy eye sees, so, in his belief, his camera sees.

But he is wrong. The eye combines in certain degrees the different offices of telescope, microscope and camera. The latter is a camera pure and simple. When we look at a landscape our eyes are continually, although unconsciously, changing their focus, and the picture ultimately conveyed to the perceptive faculty—which is a mental, not a mechanical faculty—is, in fact, not one but a succession of pictures. You are not cognisant of the fact, but before you actually perceive any view the focus of your eye has been separately adjusted to horizon, sky and clouds, far distance, middle distance and foreground. This fact and the degree of rapidity with which these adjustments are made, has its practical demonstration in that well-known optical toy, the zoetrope, or thaumatrope, in which a series of many different figures, by rapidly rotating, appear as one figure. Yet each is a distinct impression and requires its due exposure, so to speak. Therefore, even the ordinary conjurer, by his comparatively clumsy expedient of manual dexterity can easily deceive the sharpest eye. But he would not succeed in thus deceiving a photographic lens, which catches the one impression and that only, and, of course, does so in very much less time. Yet, up to a certain point although there is visual, there is no mental perception. But that point reached, these varied adjustments combine to affect the mind with one absolute, entire perception; which we call a glance, or view.

To imitate this process photographically, we should require a series of optical impressions in combination as one. But, even supposing this were possible, we should even then be farther than ever from attaining pictorial perfection, for, although we should have a view in which the geometrical perspective was complete, the details of each object near and far would give us even the most minute details, details invisible to the naked eye, for every part of the "picture" would be equally and microscopically sharp. Aerial perspective would therefore be altogether falsified. The eye, consequently, is not identical in principle with the camera.

Again a landscape photograph, examined through a microscope, shows how wonderfully perfect even its most minute details are. A landscape painting has no such quality. It was the painter's business to represent what he saw, not what was actually before him; visible effect, not invisible influences by which it was produced. It is, therefore, certain that in the act of observing, the mind is at any given fraction of a second affected and occupied by one definite *conscious* perception, the

K

result of a combination of *unconscious* impressions.

This is true, also, in another way, to which I have referred briefly in some previous chapters. If you direct your attention to any part of a view, near or distant, or to any object in it—say, a tree—instantly you have lost the specific effect of the whole, and the tree only is seen, and as a whole in itself, not as a part of the view. In like way, if you fix your attention upon the bark of the tree, or a bough of it, or one of its leaves, each of these immediately becomes a whole, to the exclusion of all the other parts. As your mind reverts to the general scene, all these details merge into one general effect; details no longer obtrude themselves as dominating factors. Now, the artist aims to represent the entire view as it affects his mind, or as he perceives it, not as an optical imstrument sees it. But the photographer, unless he, too, is an artist, aims to get what he calls sharpness in the details, and as this can only be obtained by sacrificing breadth, pictorial truth, and aerial and linear perspective, he cheerfully and contentedly, although unconsciously, destroys them all at one fell swoop.

It is his work that misleads art critics, who know nothing of the power a photographer has to modify such conditions, and causes them to denounce and ridicule photographic art claims altogether. Truth-loving artists do not, however, as some now-a-days suppose, overlook the value of details, or in any degree depreciate their importance. They simply regard them as elements in the production of general effects. They do not make them unduly prominent, but neither do they clumsily seek to realise the impossible, that wonderful and indefinite minuteness of nature, which only the microscope can fully realise.

"Why has not a man a microscopic eye?
For this good reason, man is not a fly."

Again, look at the question from another suggestive view-point. A good architectural perspective representation of any edifice gives the minutest detail of the ornamental mouldings and decorations that it is possible for mechanical skill to delineate, not for the sake of pictorial effect, but to serve technical purposes. Yet, the architect is scrupulously careful to give also their exact relative proportions, and if the dimensions of his drawing are not sufficiently large to permit this exactness of detail and proportion, he necessarily omits them. So in a landscape picture, as it is impossible to represent leaves and grass and similar natural objects with accurate details in due proportion to the scale of the entire scene, they are made subordinate to the general effect by being indicated rather than represented.

But the inartistic photographer, falsely estimating the importance of these minute details, concentrates the whole power of his lens upon their representation, and thus sacrifices relative proportions altogether, violating the rules of both linear and aerial perspective. As it is clearly an impossibility to represent leaves, blades of grass, small herbage and other minute objects, with their details distinctly visible, at the same time, in due proportion to the scale of the whole scene, such so-called exact truthfulness is productive only of unnatural results. The more conspicuous this kind of blunder is, the less truthful and interesting, and the less pictorial will be the general effect.

Nor is it any way out of this difficulty to throw the entire picture altogether out of focus—as some do—for this really only makes bad worse, for it means distortion —increases the great evil by unduly enlarging, as well as confusedly blurring forms and outlines. The only thing to be done is to so distribute the focus that, while proportion or perspective is secured, detail is not rendered unnaturally obtrusive in any part of our productions.

There is yet another view of this question. The images conveyed by the eye are very small and of one size, yet they do not appear small or of one size. Men, women, children are seemingly what we call life-size, as we seem to see them in nature ; a bush and a tree, a mole-hill and a mountain, have each their relative sizes. But when we see them on the focussing screen of a camera, or in a photograph, it is not so. It is, therefore, obvious that the images of nature undergo in some mysterious way a kind of mental enlarging process before they are mentally perceived. And in connection with this I firmly believe that the only real way of so photographing as to get anything like natural pictorial effect is to take very small and most carefully focussed negatives, on a glass made specially for them, with a view to some superior method of enlarging, of which we have already promising signs. I was struck with this the other day when a small negative was used for reproducing a life-size copy of a bust of Shakespeare, in the Memorial Library, Stratford-on-Avon—that known as the terra-cotta, or Devonshire bust—everyone who saw this regarded it as wonderful. I was also struck in the same way with the reality of aerial perspective apparent in some landscapes exhibited at the Salon, in Piccadilly, last year. They, too, were enlargements from very small negatives. Proportions, details, breadth, space, linear perspective, and aerial were all superior to anything to be found in photographs from larger negatives.

Mr. C. W. Cooke, comparing the eye with the camera, says:—" The human eye is, in fact, a *little* camera, which, by means of lenses and optical contrivances (identical in principle with, but far more perfect than, those employed in a photographic instrument) forms upon a sensitive film an image of objects to which it may be directed. The sensitive film (corresponding to the prepared collodion of the photographer) consists of a membrane at the back of the eyeball, traversed by a system of nerve-filaments of extraordinary delicacy and sensitiveness, so interlaced as to form a network, which is in consequence called the *retina*. Upon this net-work of nervous matter is thrown, by means of a lens, a *minute inverted* image of whatever the eye is directed to, and the phenomena of sight may be defined as the reading of the telegraphic message which the retina transmits through the optic nerve to the brain, descriptive of the image that is falling upon it. But, while this message is, in a healthy state of the eye, always correctly interpreted by the brain, the proverbial statement that 'seeing is believing' has, like every other rule, its exceptions." In connection with this statement, it is curious to remember that, although the eye sees the images inverted, we are not conscious of their being so.

Another view of our subject demanding consideration is found in the concentration of colours and the intensification of light and shade perceptible in camera images, as compared with those of the eye. As these mean intensified chemical action on the prepared plates, it is obvious that degrees of contrast are thereby intensified, and that a mere photograph is not true in its relative proportions or scale of light and shade. This, again, enforces the lesson I have in view, that of endeavouring to represent nature as the eye sees it, rather than as it is when conveyed to the eye by some optical instrument. Here the processes of exposing, printing and developing, call for modifications in practice. If they are conducted blindly and ignorantly by operators as mechanical as their tools, perspective and pictorial truths will be conspicuous by absence. If the good work is done by students of nature and art, who are thoroughly in earnest, we shall have photographic work steadily becoming higher in its meanings, deeper in feeling, and wider in its influences, work in which the difficulties I have been writing about in this and the preceding chapters, have been met and conquered by intellectual superiority.

I have been told recently that my tendency in writing for photographers is to aim so high that ordinary practitioners cannot follow me. Artists will smile at this, for I have not as yet advanced beyond what every art student knows to be mere elementary study, the lesson every beginner is supposed to have mastered before more weighty and abstruse matters receive attention. The photographer who turns with dismay from such simple matters has little chance of either advancing himself or his art in the estimation of critical observers.

CHAPTER XII.

BREADTH OF EFFECT.

ART critics and writers upon pictorial art have made us very familiar with such terms as breadth of effect, broad effects, broad treatment, etc., etc., but the different ways in which these words are applied, and the numerous qualities with which they are associated in practice would hardly be understood without some preliminary study. My main purpose throughout these chapters has been that of extending the views of photographic art students from mere rules and their technical methods of application to the more important principles to which such rules owe their existence, and without pretending to deal with them exhaustively illustrate their practical applications and expansibility. We now turn our attention to what is known as breadth or breadth of effect.

What this really means is not easily explained, because it means so much. All that I have written about lines, tones, perspective, accidental incidents, transitory natural effects, the phenomena of clouds, sunlight and atmosphere, etc., bear upon it in one way or another, and in degrees varying in their importance. The landscape painter I have already quoted, J. B. Pyne, in his "Nomenclature of Pictorial Art," says, "Breadth in painting is a term which denotes largeness, space, vastness. Its operation is not limited by a small canvas or extended in a large one. Finish does not preclude or negligence secure it. It very seldom accompanies mere outline, though some few and limited subjects in outline admit it. Its greatest promoters are colour and *chiaro oscuro* (lights and darks), in which, when under consummate management, it revels in full power and grandeur." This definition is that of a landscape painter. The photographer will see at once that it limits his means of securing breadth to light and shade only, although, in fact, there are many other promoters available, as further consideration of what has been already advanced will, I hope, suffice to demonstrate. In fact, all I have said and urged you to study leads up to this crowning quality of a fine picture.

If breadth means anything it certainly means the harmonious relationship of every part with the whole, a concentration of *every available power* to strengthen a given purpose. To this end the means we have had under notice all lead onward. The best composition, whether simple or complicated, is that which attains the most perfect unity, embracing outlines, *chiaro oscuro*, variety of incidents, subordination of interests and attractiveness, etc., etc., all with reference to some leading purpose, whether it be of a technical or mental sentimental or mere automatic character.

If there is *any* part of a picture that is in any way incongruous, if this or that episode takes a dominance that belongs to the entire incident, if the portrait is overpowered by background or accessories, if in a figure group that figure which should be least conspicuous is most prominent, if spots of light or dark, or strong staring lines lead the eye now here, now there, to this or that in succession, instead of fixing the spectator's attention upon the work as a whole, there will be a want of breadth, the great dominant purpose, the thought, being sacrificed to things which are of inferior consequence.

But let us turn to some other practical and reliable artists, who support this view, authorities every one, and note what they have to say.

In the " Memoirs of William Collins, R.A.," by the late Wilkie Collins, his son, we read, "Nothing in Mr. Collins's pictures more thoroughly testified to his study of nature, and his observations of the principles of the old masters, than the broad significant disposition of light and shade which they present to the eye, and which produces in them much of the vigour of effect

they may possess when seen from a distance. Neither their darks or lights appear, when thus viewed, as isolated, ungraceful patches, but assume, on the contrary, the appearance of a varied, harmonious whole, one shadow leading smoothly on to the next, and one light echoed at intervals by another. As a test of the power and correctness of his *chiaro oscuro*, let any of his pictures, with the exception of his earliest and immature efforts, be looked at under a dim light, when none of their individual qualities of form and colour can be plainly discerned, and it will be found that the general disposition of light and shade which is then alone visible in them, never assumes a disagreeably scattered or disjointed aspect, but preserves a grace and balance, a vastness and harmony, in its vague shapes, which attract the eye even in the absence of any definite object that it can observe. In those cases where his pictures are not within reach, any of the prints from " The Fisherman's Departure," " Rustic Hospitality," " Fetching the Doctor," " The Stray Kitten," or " Feeding the Rabbits," will be found to produce, although in an inferior degree, the same result. As regards the value of this test of the correctness and feeling of an artist's *chiaro oscuro*, its propriety must be apparent to any one who has observed the remarkable coherence and harmony of light and shade on natural objects, when they are fading in the tw light, and who consider that all art is excellent or faulty, in proportion as it gains or loses on being referred directly to nature."

And this reminds us of the great power an artist-photographer has in the printing process, of toning down too prominent lights, and lightening too prominent darks, deepening a little here by prolonged exposure, or giving a desirable retiring quality there by shortening it, none of which he would dare to do if preliminary study had not shown him when, where and how to do this, that or the other.

Chiaro oscuro is in itself a subject so complicated and so intimately associated with diversities of forms and methods of expression that I shall not attempt to deal with it more fully than I have already done, but its literature is very comprehensive, and in very few works of a practical character on painting will it be found not to be fairly, if in none of them exhaustively treated.

There is a danger to which it is desirable to call attention in seeking breadth. The subordination of parts to the whole must not be carried so far as to destroy all sense of variety, a quality of which I have spoken as desirable. To preserve the one without sacrificing the other is indeed one of the artist's difficulties in seeking breadth.

Another rule which associates itself with our present subject has also been dealt with separately. If the masses of parts are so equal as to produce

monotony, that monotony will dominantly assert itself and be destructive of breadth. The famous painter, James Barry, addressing the Royal Academy students on this subject said, "With respect to the conduct necessary to be pursued in obtaining this advantageous distribution of lights and darks in a picture, it has been observed, with good discernment, that the constant maxim of those great artists (Giorgione, Titian, Correggio, Rubens and others, great successors of Da Vinci) was to dispose all their light and dark objects after such a manner as would best contribute to their being seen with the greatest possible advantage and ease; that to attain this end they arranged them in groups and masses of lights, half lights, darks and half darks and reflexes. Of these lights and darks one was principal, the rest subordinate, and all generally cooperated to produce a totality and entireness in the work. The principal light was generally so disposed as to give the greatest lustre to that part where the action and the personages were of the greatest consequence, and where, accordingly, it was most proper to arrest the attention of the spectator. How far this light should extend depended upon the previous arrangement of the objects, and the discreet and sentimental accommodation of it to the nature of the subject ; but it is observable that by extending it too far, its comparative value is proportionately lessened. . . This principal light should as it were occupy only its own sphere, and not be repeated, yet not be without its satellites or dependants. Revivifications and echoes of it, subordinate in magnitude or force or both, should notwithstanding, by an artful concatenation, be disturbed to the circumstances of secondary importance in the other parts."

The principles here advocated may be variously applied, although Barry's definitions are those of a figure painter. He goes on to point out great works illustrative of such rules by figure painters amongst the old masters, but all he says bears upon landscape also. Dwelling by the way upon the great care a painter should devote to the intermediate tones and shades. " It is," he says, "principally owing to the judicious and happy management of the middle tints that these fierce opposite extremes of light and dark are brought to co-operate and harmonise," and judiciously adds, " It is not necessary that the middle tints should always intervene between every light and dark; on the contrary,

BREADTH OF EFFECT. 157

the *éclat*, spirit and propriety of certain parts absolutely require their being detached boldly from the light by the sole and immediate opposition of vigorous shadows or other dark tints." This is but another enforcement of my idea of always governing the application of rules by the science of principles. In other words, of never working without thinking.

Turn to another R. A. lecturer on pictorial art, John Opie, who writing of Correggio, says, " Of *chiaro oscuro* on the grandest scale, as it extends to the

regulation of the *whole* of a work, he was certainly the inventor. Antecedently to him no painter had attempted, or even imagined, the magic effect of this principle [breadth], which is strikingly predominant in all that remains of Correggio, from his widely extended cupolas to the smallest of his oil paintings; its sway was uncontrollable; parts were lightened, extended, curtailed, obscured or buried in the deepest shade, in compliance with its dictates; and whatever interfered (even correctness of form, propriety of action, and characteristic attitude) was occasionally sacrificed. . . . Entranced, overcome by pleasing sensation, the spectator is often compelled to forget incorrectness of drawing and deficiency of expression and character."

Opie wrote before we had pictures taken by photography, and at a time when the importance of truthful and perfect accuracy was not properly appreciated, as I tried to show in a former chapter. The lesson conveyed by Correggio's sacrificing so much for attaining breadth is not the less useful here, because it shows that even so philosophical a thinker and so accomplished a painter regarded breadth as the crowning excellence of his works. Opie and most of his best known contemporaries often sacrificed to rules qualities by no means inconsistent with the principles such rules were invented to enforce, as Constable practically demonstrated.

I might easily refer to Fuzeli, Sir Joshua Reynolds and many other great artists, ancient and modern, who have written on this subject, and show how each contributes to our knowledge of breadth, explaining its power and expansiveness as a principle, and the diversity of conclusions which have been arrived at without any real contradictions or inconsistencies, but I have perhaps already said enough to impress my pupils with a sense of its importance, and must now prepare to say good-bye.

The three examples which illustrate this chapter blend figures, architecture, sky and water into one harmonious whole very charmingly and serve well to show how the best effects in this way are obtained when accidental combinations exclude both very light and very dark extremes. In nature such happy results are not uncommon, but the exaggerations of vulgar photographs too often destroy them through under-exposure or insufficient development, the operator believing that this bold exaggeration, which is destructive of both variety and breadth, gives what he calls "brilliancy," that is, a staring out of violently contrasting patches. A point of light as focus rendered prominent by the close proximity of the focus of strongest dark is something altogether unlike this. In the one we have separated prominent patches, in the other we have gradations and unity, one part leading up to another for producing some general effect. In the one the effect is natural and harmonious and beautiful, in the other it is discordant, artificial and ugly.

There are numerous ways in which landscape painters achieve this result, but they are all ways in which nature herself acts. For instance, clouds will often, by the way in which they overshadow the entire field of view, cause all violent contrasts to at once disappear; often a little patient waiting and watching will be all that is required to catch some stray gleam of light that falls behind, say a group of trees, or cattle or cottages in deep shadow, and so create a focus which at once secures breadth and effect. Again, other always-changing cast shadows may create this desirable quality, that of a mountain for instance, or that of a forest on the slope of a hill, or that of some tall rocky sandstone cliff toning down into quiet and simple unity, the rugged projections, holes and crevices, the isolated bushes and weeds, and broken piled-up fragments, etc., each of which might otherwise assert itself too strongly for the entire combination, confusing the sight and destroying breadth of effect. Your inartistic photographer never recognises the value of subordination or breadth, his chief aim being that of rendering every object and all their details equally conspicuous, or as he says "sharp."

Of course, all this thought and care means the expenditure of time and effort. But what is even the longest time a photographer is likely to occupy in producing his picture compared with that which a painter requires! G. Barnard says whilst he was yet a tyro he was engaged in company with Stanfield and other artists in taking a sketch of the East Cliff at Hastings. He had completed his study in three hours, but Stanfield's occupied seven hours. And this sketch was in itself but a preliminary study for a finished work. Moreover, every study conducted earnestly, in a true artistic spirit, with due appreciation of both art and nature, leaves you the better and stronger for your next effort, whereas work unduly hurried is sure to be more or less slovenly work.

There is also another advantage. Armitage, in one of his lectures on painting, delivered before the students of the Royal Academy, said art progress depended not upon the efforts of individual teachers, but upon the individual exertion of every member of the profession from the president down to the probationer. "Let us all," said he, "do our best to produce careful, honest, and original work and I have no doubt of the result." Echoing these words, which are as applicable to photography and photographers as they were to the R.A. president and probationers, I too believe we need " have no doubt of the result " that follows " careful, honest and original work."

> Still, from the first, with steady pace pursue
> The winding maze of art by Nature's clue;
> For all her toils, antique or modern, tend
> But as a means to Nature, art's true end.
> Nature! the object of your search alone
> In paintings prize, and estimate in stone.
>
> . . . .
>
> Led by her light alone, in elder time
> Immortal Genius ran his course sublime
> From Glory's summit snatch'd the brightest crown,
> And rifled all the regions of renown.
>
> *Sir Martin Archer Shee, A.R.*

Figures in Keeping with a Cottage Exterior.
From a Drawing.

CHAPTER XIII.

FIGURES AND FOREGROUNDS.

THE power a photographer has in the introducing of figures of men and beasts or other movable objects into his landscape, may be exercised in a vast variety of ways and with many purposes: for example, to blot out some undesirable feature; break up a mass or line which is antagonistic to the general effect; supply

Example of Figures judiciously used in aid of the Composition.
From an Engraving.

here a focus of dark, or there one of light; carry the observer's eye into the picture to express space; lead it to the chief point of interest; tell some particular story which lends itself to the picture's chief purpose—give some human interest to a village street or a town view, or some suggestion of wild life in a wild spot; make a foreground where otherwise no foreground could be secured; introduce some aspect of domestic doing to emphasize cottage life, or the life of a country gentleman's old manor-house, castle or mansion; to secure breadth, contrast, harmony, etc., etc. The illustrations given with this chapter are all suggestive of work to

Examples of Figures judiciously used in aid of the Composition.
From Engravings.

FIGURES AND FOREGROUNDS. 165

Examples of Figures judiciously used in aid of the Composition.
From Engravings.

be done of this kind, as are, indeed, most of those already given in which figures are seen.

It may sometimes be found desirable to fill up a spot which is too staringly conspicuous, and without

other kind of importance to justify its being so prominent, and this can be done perhaps easily enough by moving a bush, the trunk of a felled tree, some broken or displaced boughs, transplanted weeds, a pile

Examples of Figures judiciously used in aid of the Composition.
From Engravings.

of fragments from rocks and boulders thrown together in some naturally suggestive way, and so on and so on. The ingenuity of the artist will readily help him in such matters, and these mere hints will suffice.

FIGURES AND FOREGROUNDS.

Use of Figures with a Low Horizon.

Figures Securing Balance in the Composition.

A Simple Effective Foreground.

Figures and Landscape.   From an old painting.

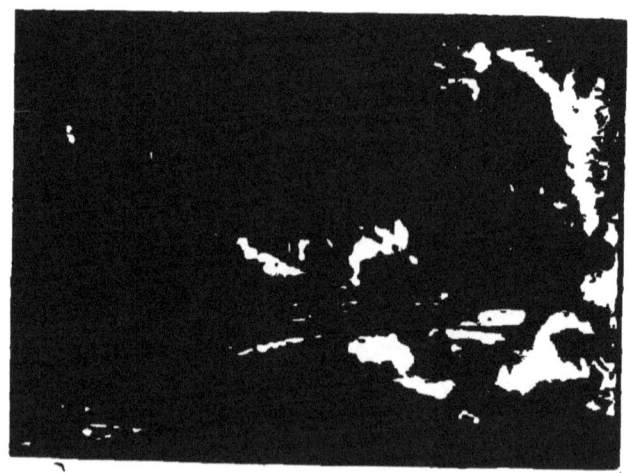

A Foreground Effect.   From a Lithograph.

CHAPTER XIV.

GOOD HINTS FROM GOOD AUTHORITIES OLD AND NEW.

"In all picture compositions the thought should take the first place, and all else be regarded as the language which is to give it expression."—*O. G. Rejlander, Artist and Photographer.*

"Tell your story, describe your scene, express your sentiments, or display your learning in words, but do not attempt to do so in a language with which you have made yourself imperfectly acquainted."—*C. R. Leslie, R.A.*

"Nature can only suggest what stimulates the poet to the conception of a whole; and the poet must have the capacity to be so stimulated."—*Joseph Skipsey, the Miner-Poet.*

"It is not at all surprising that the success of eminent artists should tempt many who are altogether unqualified to practise art—if it only tempted them to its study it would be well for them."—*Dogmas on Art.*

"Things more excellent than every image are expressed through images."—*Jamblichus.*

"Upon the choice of a proper and judicious distance—meaning the distance intervening between the spectator's position and that point on the ground directly in front of him, where the picture that he is about to take ought properly to commence—the beauty of the artist's work will in a great measure depend.—*Thomas Rowbotham, Landscape Painter.*

"The young student should in the first place acquire a knowledge of perspective to enable him to give every object its proper dimensions, after which it is requisite that he be under the care of an able master. . . . Next he must study nature in order to confirm and fix in his mind the reason of those precepts which he has learnt."—*Leonardo da Vinci.*

"With a short focus lens it is impossible to obtain any true foreshortening, and every photographer gets so accustomed to this false perspective that he accepts without a thought of objection effects that would drive an artist wild. . . . The man who studies art *after* learning the *science* of photography is handicapped, he is apt to be misled by scientific and optical limitation, and to accept the result of those limitations as truths."
—*G. Hanmer Croughton, Photographer.*

"Ought not sound criticism to look to results only, and to disregard the means employed, and the precise amount of difficulty overcome in producing them? I think that a careful study of the work of painters, so far as composition is concerned, will show that pictorially the photographer may justly claim far more latitude in the choice of subject and the way of representing it than many fancy themselves entitled to, and a result of realizing this fact and acting upon it, would introduce a greater variety in the work produced by camera and lens—a result to be devoutly wished."—*Rev. T. Perkins,* in the *Amateur Photographer.*

"Sky effects of some sort or another, the photographic beginner must have in his pictures if he is to represent, in ever so poor a degree, *anything* of the spirit of a scene."—*Rev. A. H. Blake, M.A., Photographer.*

" Place any number of artists or amateurs before a given subject, and the sketch or painting or photograph of each will not show so much what the limitation of material was, as it will be an expression of the perception of each."—*Horace Markley, Photographer, in the Art Interchange.*

" Not a few photographers have the idea that the laws of composition are formulæ whereby pictures can be made. This is no more the case than the laws of syntax and prosody are receipts for making poetry. If pictures were made like puddings, by receipt, there would be no art required."—*The Amateur Photographer.*

" The student may at first feel disheartened at his ill success in the imitation of nature, but whatever he does in obedience to her precepts will be infinitely superior to anything which he himself could conceive. . . . All standard rules are useless without constant study in the school of nature."—*J. W. Carmichael, Marine Painter.*

A Selection from the Publications of Percy Lund & Co., Ltd.

Burton's Manual of Photography.

By W. K. BURTON. C.E. A practical handbook for all who are taking up photography. An explicit guide to all ordinary photographic manipulations. The latest information. With examples of the author's own work. Contents: The Dark Room—Filling the Dark Slides—The Camera in the Field—Portraits—Groups—Flashlight Photography — Instantaneous Photography — Developing, Fixing, Intensifying and Reducing Plates—Over and Under-exposure—Tentative Development—Various kinds of Developers—Defects and Remedies—Printing on Gelatino-Chloride Paper—On Ready Sensitized Albumenized Paper—By the Platinotype Process—By the Kallitype Process and the Carbon Process—and on Bromide Paper—Varnishing Negatives—Trimming and Mounting Prints—Vignetting—Printing-in Skies—Soft Prints from Ordinary Negatives—Orthochromatic or Isochromatic Plates—Transparencies or Diapositives—Lantern Slides. 184 pages, well illustrated. Paper covers, 1/0 net.

"From Mr. W. K. Burton's pen we naturally expect to get nothing but good work."

Practical Essays on Art.

By JOHN BURNET.
I.—PRACTICAL HINTS ON COMPOSITION. Contents:—Composition—Angular Composition—Circular Composition.
II.—PRACTICAL HINTS ON LIGHT AND SHADE. Seven full-page plates, with descriptive letterpress, given in this essay.
III.—THE EDUCATION OF THE EYE. Contents: Measurement—Form—Perspective—Lines—Diminution—Angles—Circles—Aërial Perspective.

130 illustrations, including examples by Cuyp, Rubens, Potter, Ostade, Claude, Metzu, P. de Laer, Wouvermans, Raffaelle, Dominichino, Rembrandt, Gerard Douw, Correggio, Michael Angelo, and other eminent masters. Crown 4to. Red cloth, 132 pages, 2/6 net; post-free, 2/10½.

The Elements of a Pictorial Photograph.

By H. P. ROBINSON. Demy 8vo, half bound, with 37 pictures in the text and frontispiece, "Storm Clearing Off." 3/6 net. Dedicated to the Brothers of the Linked Ring, whose efforts have done much towards saving the art of photography from extinction. Synopsis of Chapters: Introduction—Imitation—The Study of Nature—The Use of Nature—Some Points of a Picture—Selection and Suppression — Composition — Expression in Landscape — Idealism, Realism and Impressionism—Limitations. The Nude—False Purity—The Question of Focus—Models—Foregrounds—The Sky—The Sea—Rural Subjects—Lessons from Birket Foster—Winter Photography—Individuality—Conclusion.

PERCY LUND & CO., LTD.,

The Country Press, Bradford; and
Memorial Hall, Ludgate Circus, E.C.

The Lund Library of Photography.

In Two-Shilling Volumes, net.

Cloth bound. A series of text-books devoted to the branches and applications of photography. Plain wording and explicit teaching is aimed at as far as possible.

The Stereoscope and Stereoscopic Photography.

Translated from the French of F. DROUIN by MATTHEW SURFACE. Principal Contents: Binocular Vision—The Perception of Relief—Various Forms of Stereoscopes—Applications of Stereoscope — Stereoscopic Photography — Stereoscopic Negatives — Stereoscopic Prints, etc. 180 pages. More than 100 illustrations.

"The information given as to the various forms of stereoscopes is very complete. The book is well illustrated by numerous diagrams and process blocks."—*Amateur Photographer*.

Photographic Lenses: How to Choose and How to Use.

By JOHN A. HODGES. An elementary and Practical Guide to the selection and use of Photographic Objectives. Contents: Optical Principles—Definition of Terms—Various Defects in Lenses—The Diaphragm or Stop, and its Functions—Single Lenses—Upon the Properties and Use of Single Lenses—The Rapid Rectilinear, or Non-Distorting Doublet—Other Forms of the Doublet, including Wide-Angle Lenses—Portrait and Universal Lenses—New Types of Lenses, Constructed of Jena Glass—On certain Obsolete Lenses —Upon the Choice of a Lens—The Care of Lenses—Upon Focussing—Upon Angle of View—Distortion: and its avoidance by the Use of the Swing Back—Combination Lenses, Casket Lenses, and the Use of Back Combinations—How to Test a Lens—Lenses of Foreign Construction — On Purchasing Second-hand Lenses— Dallmeyer's Tele-photographic Lenses. 148 pages and 36 original illustrations, including eight half-tone engravings.

Photography for Artists.

By HECTOR MACLEAN. Contents: The Extent to which Photography is used by Artists—Concerning Various Kinds of Artists' Studies—The Right to Copy Artists' Studies—Photographic Reproductions of Works of Art—Some Photographic Falsities— The Photographic Misrepresentation of Tones—Falsifications in Photographic Printing—Some Reasons why Artists should Use a Camera—The Choice and Use of Apparatus, etc., suitable for Artists —Indoor Photography; Models, Sitters, Copying Pictures—On the Reproduction of Pictures—Illustrations for Photographic Reproduction—Condensed List of Photographs for Artists—List of Reference Books. 152 pages, with an appendix consisting of 16 pages illustrations, besides 19 diagrams and illustrations in the text.

"A temperately written, useful little manual this."—*The Studio*.
"It should be a book of real practical value to all those who look upon photography not jealously as a rival, but as an honourable ally, in whom artists of all sorts may find a trustworthy and helpful friend."—*The Studio*.

The Lund Library of Photography.—*Continued.*

The Half-Tone Process.

By JULIUS VERFASSER. A Practical Manual of Photo-Engraving in Half-Tone on Zinc and Copper. Second edition: revised and in great part re-written. Contents: What is Half-Tone?—The Studio and its Fittings—The Camera—The Screen—The Dark-room — The Printing-room — The Etching-Room — The Mounting Room—Negative Making—Failures and Remedies in Negative Making—Printing from the Negative—The Etching—Mounting and Proving. 172 pages and 75 illustrations, with four supplement illustrations in half-tone by the author.

"This clear and concise demonstration of half-tone process, as evolved by Mr. Verfasser, is sufficient, in our opinion, to give any ordinary intelligent person a very good notion of the general principle involved.—*Invention.*

Half-Tone on the American Basis.

From the personal experience of WILHELM CRONENBERG. Translated by WILLIAM GAMBLE. Chapters on Photo-Engraving in America—Apparatus for Negative Making—The Negative—Stripping and Reversing the Negative—The Printing Process—Etching—Finishing Work—Engraving—Vignettes. 56 illustrations in the text, and twelve supplementary on art paper at end of book. 164 pages.

"The work strikes us as being especially valuable on account of the fulness with which it treats of the apparatus employed in which respect it has the advantage of other books on Half-Tone that we have read."—*British Journal of Photography.*

Plates and Papers: How Made and Used.

By Dr. H. C. STIEFEL Giving instructions how to make Albumen, Gelatine, Collodion, Platinum, Carbon and other Papers, and how to Print, Tone, Develop and Fix the Pictures upon them, based upon practical experience in the factory and studio. Contents: The Dark Room—Dry Plates—Developing Dry Plates Paramidophenol, Rodinal, Metol, Eikonogen, Amidol, etc.—Fixing—Orthochromatic Dry Plates—The "Gelatine" Hardness—Paper—Albumen—Albumen Paper—Sensitizing Albumen Paper—Collodion—Sensitized Collodion Emulsion—Preparing Collodion Paper—Coating Collodion Paper by Machinery—Printing, Toning and Fixing—Gelatine—Gelatine Sensitized Paper—Coating Paper with Gelatine Emulsion—Coating Gelatine Paper by Machinery—Printing and Toning Gelatine Papers—Combined Baths—Developing Prints upon Printing-out Paper—Mounting—Plain Matt Surface Paper—Matt Surface Collodion and Gelatine Papers—Blue Prints (Cyanotype)—Platinum Paper—Kallitype Paper—Bromide Paper Developing Bromide Paper—Diazotype, or Primuline Process—Bichromate of Potassium Printing Process—Chromatype Process—Carbon Tissue. 200 pages, with several illustrations.

PERCY LUND & CO., LTD.,

The Country Press, Bradford; and
Memorial Hall, Ludgate Circus, E.C.

Devoted to Photography, Artistic and Scientific.

Price Threepence.

Devoted to the subjects of photography, artistic and scientific, photographic processes, and the utility of photography in connection with other arts and sciences. The latest discoveries and advances are recorded in its pages. The leading writers of our times contribute to its columns, and the past few numbers have contained articles by the following:—

COL STEWART.
H. P. ROBINSON.
GEO. E. THOMPSON.
A. H. WALL.
GAMBIER BOLTON.
ANDREW YOUNG.
HECTOR MACLEAN.
REV. T. PERKINS.

JULIUS VERFASSER.
H. J. L. J. MASSÉ.
ARTHUR BURCHETT.
E. MACDOWEL COSGRAVE, M.D.
GEO. G. ROCKWOOD.
HAROLD BAKER.
SIR W. M. CONWAY.

Etc., etc.

Descriptive Biographies.

A series of Descriptive Biographies of some of our leading photographers has been continued at frequent intervals for some time past. Among others the following have been interviewed and their work described:—

H. P. ROBINSON.
J. PATTISON GIBSON.
ALFRED WERNER.
GEO. E. THOMPSON.
ANDREW YOUNG.
JOHN AND ROBERT TERRAS.

ARTHUR RESTON.
F. BOISSONNAS.
ADAM DISTON.
DRINKWATER BUTT.
J. CRAIG ANNAN.
W. PARRY.

The Notes

are a prominent feature, and comprise various items of interest coming under the heads of **Under the Sun, Editorial Focus, Practical Work, Novelties and Business Items, Literature, Photographs of the Month,** etc. From a pictorial point of view *The Practical Photographer* takes a high position. There are varied Frontispieces or Supplement Illustrations every month, in half-tone, or other processes, besides many pictures in the text. In this line, indeed, the magazine leaves behind many higher-priced publications. It is largely supported by professional and scientific photographers in all parts of the world, and many practical men are regular contributors to its columns.

PERCY LUND & CO., LTD.,

The Country Press, Bradford ; and Memorial Hall, Ludgate Circus, E.C.

www.ingramcontent.com/pod-product-compliance
Lightning Source LLC
Chambersburg PA
CBHW031451160426
43195CB00010BB/929